9-26-75

Goodheart-Willcox's BUILD-A-COURSE Series

metalworking

by

T. GARDNER BOYD

Director, Career & Continuing Education
Public Schools, Kansas City, Missouri

WALTER C. BROWN, Consulting Editor

Professor, Division of Technology
Arizona State University, Tempe

Books in Build-A-Course Series

Metalworking — Boyd	Graphic Arts — Kagy
Woodworking — Wagner	Power Mechanics — Atteberry
Drafting — Brown	Leathercraft — Zimmerman
Electricity — Gerrish	Ceramics — Brennan
Electronics — Gerrish	Plastics — Cope
Art Metals — Siegner	Modern General Shop

South Holland, Illinois

THE GOODHEART-WILLCOX COMPANY, INC.
Publishers

INTRODUCTION

This book is one of a series planned specifically to provide general exploratory experiences in Industrial Arts. It is designed to provide a broad experience in METALWORKING through the use of tools, machines, and materials that are basic to this important area.

The book includes informational topics, general careers information, planning and designing, safety, bench metal, sheet metal, forging, welding, founding, heat treating, and machine shop. Although some shops may not be equipped to teach all the areas presented, students will have an opportunity to read about the several areas of metalwork.

Hand tool operations are stressed since this course is designed for the student who is beginning his study of metalwork, or has had very little experience in this area. Each unit progresses from the use of simple hand tools to some of the more basic machine operations, so the student can gain the necessary background of information and skill needed, as he progresses to more advanced metalworking.

A number of shop-tested projects are presented which will help stimulate interest and provide a challenge. The projects range from simple projects to some which are more complex.

The author hopes that this book will contribute to the student's knowledge and skill needed for everyday living, as well as his pursuit of career and avocational interests.

T. Gardner Boyd

Copyright 1975 by
THE GOODHEART-WILLCOX CO., INC.

Previous Editions Copyright 1968, 1964, 1961
No part of this book may be reproduced in any form without violating the copyright law. Printed in U.S.A. Library of Congress Catalog Card Number 74–23306. International Standard Book Number 0–87006–187–9.

123456789–75–0987654

Library of Congress Cataloging in Publication Data

Boyd, T   Gardner.
  Metalworking.

  (Goodheart-Willcox's build-a-course series)
  Bibliography: p.
  Includes index.
  1. Metal-work.   I.   Title.
TT205.B68   1975   684'.09   74–23306
ISBN 0–87006–187–9

CONTENTS

METAL IN OUR EVERYDAY LIVES

UNIT 1

SOME ANSWERS TO THESE QUESTIONS:

1. Why should you study metalwork?
2. What does the future hold for metal-working industries and employment?
3. What career opportunities are available in the areas of metalwork and related fields?

A CHAT WITH YOUR TEACHER

The metalworking industries and their products play an important part in the lives of all of us. Through metal products our homes have been made more comfortable, sanitary, and convenient places to live. Our modes of transportation have become more luxurious and convenient with automobiles, streamlined trains, and jet airplanes.

Metals and metal alloys have played a very important part in the development of rockets and satellites. Metal undoubtedly will play an ever increasing roll as space ships and other items are developed for our adventures to other planets.

We are all consumers of metal products. Our homes are filled with items made of metal such as washing machines, refrigerators, metal furniture, automobiles, bicycles, and many other products which we use every day. To be an intelligent user of these articles you should be able to recognize good design and quality craftsmanship. The skills you learn in metalwork will help you as a consumer and will also enable you to repair and maintain many of these metal products. You may also develop a fascinating hobby making useful articles of metal.

METALS IN THE FUTURE

As we look into the future it is possible to visualize still further progress in the utilization of metal, especially when we consider our vast mining resource, huge steel mills, refining plants, and the progress our scientists are making in the development of new metal alloys. America's entry into the space age will create thousands of new and interesting jobs. In order to keep pace with the new developments in the aircraft, missile, and spacecraft field as well as our everyday needs, increasing numbers of engineers, scientists, technicians, and skilled craftsmen will be needed.

A recent census report reveals that more than 10 percent of the people in our country are directly or indirectly engaged in some phase of the metalworking field. There are many different career and job offerings in each area of metalwork. Industry needs engineers and skilled technicians to plan and supervise the work. Skilled craftsmen are needed to perform the more difficult machining and fabricating operations. Semi-skilled people are needed to operate production machines, and to do the many routine jobs.

CAREER OPPORTUNITIES

As you study the various areas of metalworking included in this book you will want to explore and become aware of the many exciting career opportunities that are available in this interesting field of work. While studying the metalworking careers you should find the answers to these questions:

1. What are the working conditions?
2. Is this the kind of work I will enjoy doing?
3. What kind of training or educational qualifications will be required?
4. Do I have the mental ability to complete the training successfully?
5. Can I meet the physical requirements?
6. What are the employment trends in this field of work?
7. What are the economic returns, including salary range, possibilities for promotion, vacations, sick leave, and retirement?

	Careers		Careers
Bench Metal	Basic To All Metalwork	Heating Treating	Heat Treater
	Bench Repairman		Casehardener
	Ornamental Iron Worker		Tool Hardener
	Iron Worker, Shop Riveter		Checker
			Material Tester
Forging	Tool Dresser		Furnace Man
	Hammersmith		Temperer
	Blacksmith		
	Spring Maker	Machine Shop	Machinist
	Hand Drop Hammer		Machine Shop Foreman
	Operator		Tool Supervisor
	Forging Press Operator		Machinist, Bench
	Angle Press Operator		Instrument Maker
	Bolt Machine Operator		Tool and Die Maker
			Tool Maker
Foundry	Bench Molder		Engine Lathe Operator
	Finish Molder		Milling Machine
	Machine Molder		Operator
	Chief Inspector		
	Die Casting Machine	Sheet Metal	Sheet Metal Worker
	Operator		Sheet Metal Layout Man
	Coremaker		Furnace Sheet Metal
	Blast Furnace Keeper		Worker
	Electric Arc Furnace		Construction Sheet
	Operator		Metal Worker
	Sand Control Man		Sheet Metal Foreman
	Ladle Man		Template Layout Man

Fig. 1-1. Career opportunities in the fields of metalwork.

CAREER INFORMATION SOURCES

Each unit of study in METALWORKING has an overview of career opportunities pertaining to the area. However, you may want to do additional research and study about some of the metalworking industries in which you are interested. Your library may have some of the following publications, however, if they are not available your teacher can help you obtain them:

American Iron and Steel Institute, 150 East 42nd Street, New York, New York 10017.

American Society of Heating, Refrigeration and Air Conditioning Engineers, Inc., 345 East 47th Street, New York, New York 10017.

American Society of Mechanical Engineers, 345 East 47th Street, New York, New York 10017.

American Welding Society, 345 East 47th Street, New York, New York 10017.

Forging Industry Association, 55 Public Square, Cleveland, Ohio 44113

International Association of Machinists, 1300 Connecticut Avenue, N.W., Washington, D.C. 20036.

National Tool, Die and Precision Machinery Manufacturers Association, 907 Public Square Building, Cleveland, Ohio 44113.

Occupational Outlook Handbook, United States Government Printing Office, Washington, D.C. 20402.

Sheet Metal and Air Conditioning Contractors National Association, Inc., 107 Center Street, Elgin, Illinois 60120.

United Association of Journeymen, Apprentices, of Plumbing and Pipe Fitting Industries, 901 Massachusetts Avenue, N.W., Washington, D.C. 20001.

Fig. 1-1, lists areas of metalwork covered in this book, and a partial list of occupational classifications that offer excellent paying jobs.

It is impractical to offer, in the school shop, training in all of the specific careers listed in Fig. 1-1, so our course will be concerned with the <u>basic skills</u> involved in the various areas.

As you study this book and explore the various areas by constructing the projects you design, or those described in the Project Section, you will discover which areas you like best. If you enjoy metalwork and do well in your work, you should give serious thought to taking up some phase of metalwork as your vocation.

The aircraft industries provide many careers in the sheet metal trades and other skilled crafts. (Cessna Aircraft Co.)

DESIGNING METALWORKING PROJECTS

UNIT 2

1. Importance of good design.
2. Basic principles of good design.
3. Why it is necessary to know about materials used in metalwork when designing metal projects.

GOOD DESIGN

Design is more important in our every day lives than we sometimes realize. Did you ever stop to think about the part it played in the development and construction of the home you live in, and the furniture you use? Cars, airplanes, and rockets have all been developed from drawings on paper. Many of these products are pleasing in looks; some are not. You will want to learn to sense and recognize the good qualities in design so you can be a good judge of consumer products.

Our great industrial development has been successful largely because new and better ideas for products, processes, and machines are constantly being developed. Probably one of the biggest reasons the United States has become the leading nation in the world, is because each of us want new, different, and better products. To keep ahead, our country needs people who can think seriously and creatively for themselves.

CAREER OPPORTUNITIES

There are many excellent careers in the design field. They range from jobs as design draftsmen to design engineers. A designer creates or draws designs for the construction of articles. He may develop designs for machinery, apparatus or equipment. The designer draws up construction details, determines production methods, and standards of performance. A design engineer, for example, checks designs to see if the items can be constructed with the manufacturing equipment available. If new equipment is needed, he checks its availability and cost. A tool designer develops tool designs, jigs, and special fixtures for a specific function, and he frequently redesigns tools to improve their efficiency. He must

have a background of knowledge in machine shop practice, drafting, shop mathematics, and characteristics of the materials to be used. As you pursue this metalworking course you will have an opportunity to perform some of the jobs of a designer.

DESIGNING YOUR PROJECT

You can learn to design as you develop the projects you build in metalwork. Designing begins with a problem. It may be to invent and create a new product or to improve one that is already in use. Typical questions you will want to answer regarding the designing of your project are:

1. What is it for? What is the purpose of the project and what must it do?
2. Are there any limitations involved? For example, if you are not allowed to use certain machines, can all parts be made without them? Other limitations might be the availability of materials or processes to be used.
3. Has the problem been solved by others, if so, how can it be improved? Can it be designed to meet your particular needs?

After you can answer these questions satisfactorily your next step is to:

1. Make several freehand sketches of your ideas so they can be studied by you and your teacher. While studying your sketches, consider several different designs of the project and the kind of material to be used for each part.
2. Make desirable changes. Then, make a working drawing which can be used to guide your construction of the project. Also make full-scale drawings of the parts which have irregular shapes.

7

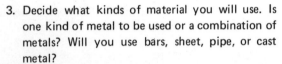

Fig. 2-1. Combinations of lines are used to
form shapes.

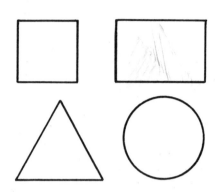

Fig. 2-2. Four basic shapes.

3. Decide what kinds of material you will use. Is one kind of metal to be used or a combination of metals? Will you use bars, sheet, pipe, or cast metal?
4. Plan the procedure you will follow to construct your project.

As you design projects you will need to consider certain basic elements and principles that make up the over-all design of an article. Study the following basic elements and principles of design:

1. Line. All things we can see have line. Buildings, cars, trees, flowers, and birds are all made up of lines, Fig. 2-1. There are three principal types of line--straight, curved, and circular. These lines when properly combined give an article a pleasing shape.
2. Shape. There are four basic shapes--square, rectangular, triangular, and round, Fig. 2-2. You see these shapes, or a combination of these shapes, when you look at nature, or man-made objects. Shape is influenced by function.
3. Mass or Solid. The solid shape or outline of an object has dimensions of thickness, width, and height. When you look at an object the mass may be square, round, or some other geometric form, Fig. 2-3. You will use rods, bars, cubes and sheets of metal in developing your projects to make up a Mass or Solid shape.
4. Proportion. The relationship between dimensions is called proportion. This relationship may be as a ratio. The "golden rule" is a proportion of about 5 to 8. Odd ratios such as 3 to 5, 7 to 9, 9 to 11 are usually preferable. Rectangles, ovals,

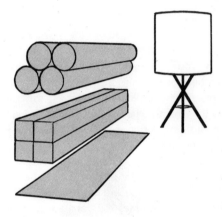

Fig. 2-3. Rods, bars, and sheets of metal are used to make up a larger shape or mass.

and free forms are more pleasing as a rule than are squares and circles, Fig. 2-4.
5. Balance. An object has balance when its parts appear to be of equal weight--neither top heavy, nor bottom heavy, nor lopsided. There are two kinds of balance:
Symmetrical Balance--When the parts on each side of the center are alike in shape and size, Fig. 2-5 (A).
Informal Balance--when the design is such that the balance cannot be measured or laid out with a ruler, and yet you get the feeling that it is balanced, Fig. 2-5 (B). Informal balance is usually more interesting than symmetrical balance.
6. Unity. A design that has unity seems to bring the various parts together as a whole. Each part of the object seems to have a relationship and your

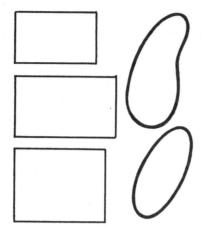

Fig. 2-4. Rectangles and free forms.

Fig. 2-6. Emphasis is brought out through shape, color, or decorations.

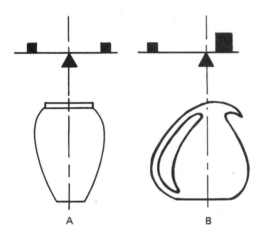

Fig. 2-5 (A) Symmetrical balance. (B) Informal balance.

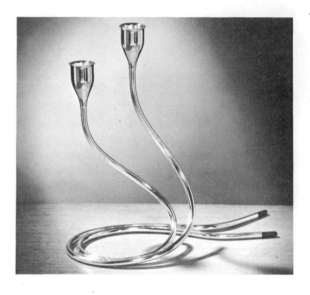

Fig. 2-7. In these candlesticks lines and curves are repeated to create rhythm.

eyes follow through and among the various parts with ease.

7. Emphasis. The design is given a point of interest. A certain part of the object may stand out through the use of color, its shape or the way it is decorated, Fig. 2-6.

8. Rhythm. Rhythm is achieved by repeating lines, curves, forms, colors, and the textures within the design. It gives an object a feeling of movement and a pleasing appearance, Fig. 2-7.

9. Harmony. Harmony results when the different parts of a design fit and look well together, Fig. 2-8. Too much harmony can make a design monotonous and uninteresting. Variety is then needed to make it more pleasing.

10. Texture. Texture is the condition of the surface of a material. Many metals have texture ranging

Fig. 2-8. In this design, harmony is obtained by using parts that fit and look well together.

9

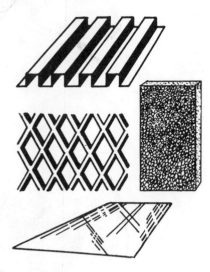

Fig. 2-9. Texture can be added by hammering, perforating, cutting, or forming the metal.

from a smooth to a very coarse surface. Texture can be added by perforating, cutting, pressing, rolling, or expanding, Fig. 2-9. When applying texture to your design be sure it is appropriate to the article, and to its function.

11. Color. All metals have a color of their own. For example, aluminum is silvery, while copper is a rich reddish brown. Colors may also be added by using lacquer, paint, chemicals, or other finishing materials. The selection of color is important in any design. Colors must be chosen carefully, or they may ruin a perfectly good project. Ordinarily, one color should be dominant in the design. The main color should be appropriate for the project. The qualities of colors should be considered. Some colors, such as red, orange, and yellow have warmth while other colors, such as blue, purple, and green are cool.

SELECTION OF MATERIALS

In order to design and construct quality projects in metal work, you will need to become familiar with some of the more common materials used. It will be necessary for you to know something about the various properties of metal and the shapes and sizes available.

Metal is one of the most common elements found on earth. Some of the metals mined are: aluminum, copper, gold, silver, and iron. You have probably heard someone speak of an alloy. An alloy is a combination of two or more metals melted and mixed together in certain proportions. For example, brass is a metal alloy which is produced by mixing copper and zinc. The properties of base metals and metal alloys vary widely. Among these properties are:

1. Hardness, the resistance to surface abrasion or penetration. Metal becomes harder as it is worked (by hammering on it) and by heat treating (explained in Unit 8). The harder the metal, the less likely it is to bend or change shape. Hard metals are more brittle than soft metals.
2. Malleability, the ability to be shaped by rolling out or hammering when cold.
3. Ductility, the ability to undergo deformation (change of shape) without breaking.
4. Elasticity, the ability to return to the original shape after deformation.
5. Fatigue Resistance, the ability to resist repeated small stresses.

The metals you will use for projects will come under the following classifications:

1. Ferrous Metal (made from iron)
   a. Low-carbon steel which is often called mild steel, contains about 0.15 to 0.30 percent carbon. This is not enough carbon to harden the steel to any appreciable degree. This type of steel may be purchased in sheets, bars, and rods. It is easily formed, machined, and welded. You will use low-carbon steel for some of the projects you construct in bench metal work.
   b. Medium-carbon steel contains about 0.30 to 0.60 percent carbon. This type of steel works well for parts of projects which require machining.
   c. High-carbon steel contains from 0.60 to .100 percent carbon. It is sometimes referred to as tool steel. Most school shops use high-carbon steel that has about 0.90 percent carbon for chisels, punches, and similar projects, since this steel can be hardened and tempered.
2. Nonferrous Metal (made without iron)
   a. Aluminum is a bright, silver metal which is light in weight and strong. There are many alloys of aluminum but most school shops stock only the softer kind, such as 1100-0 and 3003-0 in sheets. Rods, bars, and angles

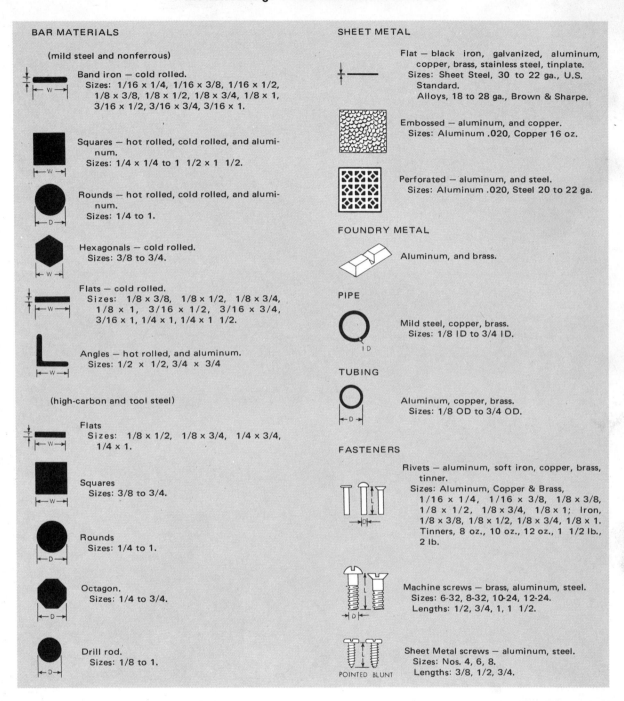

Fig. 2-10. Materials commonly used in metal work.

are used which have a harder temper. Aluminum alloys 43 and 108 are used for sand casting in the foundry. Aluminum is also used to construct bench metal, sheet metal, art metal, and machine shop projects.

b. Brass is an alloy of copper and zinc. It has a gold color. It is very ductile (may be hammered or drawn out thin) and easy to saw and file. Brass provides a very interesting color contrast when used with other metals.

c. Copper has a rich reddish brown color. It is easy to form and solder, but is hard to machine. Copper takes a beautiful polish. It is used for decorative articles such as bowls, trays, and lamps. It is also an excellent conductor of electricity.

EXOTIC METALS

You may want to do some research to find out more about some of the metals that are being used in atomic energy and space programs. Although scientists and engineers have known about these metals for some time, their use in the field of atomic energy and space programs has brought about more information concerning their characteristics of exceptional strength, rigidity, and the high temperatures they can withstand.

Beryllium, columbium, and titanium are a few of the more widely used metals in the construction of new space age craft being developed. Beryllium, for example, is lightweight and can be easily worked. It maintains good properties even at elevated temperatures. Because of the brittleness of this metal, technicians have encountered problems in forming beryllium. Although its principal use has been in alloys with copper, pure beryllium is proving to be quite useful in the field of atomic energy as a moderator and reflector in nuclear reactors. Columbium is a chemical element that has a high melting point of about 4380 deg. F. It retains good strength up to approximately 2000 deg. F. It resists the actions of most acids. Because of these characteristics, manufacturers are researching its use in the production of some space vehicle parts. Metallurgists are experimenting with the use of this metal for parts used in nuclear reactors, since it has a resistance to radiation damage. Titanium compares to low alloy steel in strength but weighs about one half as much. It can be heat treated and retains high strength up to approximately 1100 deg. F. With the development of supersonic aircraft, titanium has become important as a structural metal. Researchers are presently concerned with improving its qualities by developing protective coatings and discovering cheaper methods of processing this metal.

Many other metals are being researched, such as tantalum and tungsten, as we look for metals to be used in our atomic and space age technological developments. Tantalum is a white, ductile, malleable metal having a melting point of 5162 deg. F. Tungsten is silver white in color, ductile, and has a melting point of 6116 deg. F, which is higher than any other metal. The future use of these metals should be very exciting.

COMMON SHAPES AND SIZES OF METAL

Choosing the correct metal for your project is very important. The proper size must be selected so your finished project will be strong, durable, and meet all of the principles of good design. Study Fig. 2-10, to become familiar with the various shapes, sizes, and characteristics of the more common metals. Fig. 2-10, also shows the most common metal fasteners. Become familiar with them so you can decide the best way to fasten the parts of your project together.

QUIZ — Unit 2

Write answers on separate sheet of paper. Do not write in book.

1. How will the study of design help you as a consumer?
2. List three things to consider when designing a project _____, _____, and _____.
3. What do the basic elements of design, line and shape have in common?
4. The solid shape or outline of an object has dimensions of _____ ,_____, and _____.
5. The relationship between dimensions is called _____.
6. Rectangles, ovals, and free forms are more pleasing as a rule than, _____ and _____.
7. Explain the difference between symmetrical balance and informal balance.
8. What is the purpose of emphasis in designing a project?
9. Texture can be added to metal by _____, _____, _____, or _____.
10. List five properties of metals.
11. Ferrous metal is made from _____.
12. Nonferrous metal is made from _____.
13. High carbon steel contains from _____ to _____ percent carbon.
14. Medium carbon steel works well for parts of a project requiring machining. (True or False?)
15. Brass is an alloy of _____ and _____.

METAL SHOP SAFETY

1. **The importance of a proper attitude toward safety.**
2. **Safety guides for dressing properly.**
3. **How to use metalworking tools safely.**
4. **Good housekeeping safety guides.**

"Hi! I'm Sammy Safety. My ambition is to help you learn to work safely with tools, machines, and other equipment found in shops, and around the home so you won't get hurt. Injuries are painful and can be very serious. Many accidents occur because people are not informed. My job is to keep you informed and warn you when there is danger involved.

Study this lesson thoroughly and learn the safety guides listed. Watch for me as you study other lessons. I will be around to keep you informed and remind you about safety.

The proper safe attitude is very important in preventing accidents. This attitude is developed by accepting the guides and rules described in this book and demonstrated by your teacher. Safe practices and proper methods are for you, and not just the other fellow's. You are not a "sissy" if you wear goggles and use guards — you are smart. Just remember the right way is the safe way.

A football uniform is designed to overcome some of the hazards of the game. You know the dangers in playing the game without being properly dressed. The same holds true for the metalworker. While working in the metals area always dress properly for the job to be done and follow these guides:

1. Roll your sleeves above your elbows.
2. Remove your tie or tuck it in your shirt.
3. Remove wrist watch, rings and other pieces of jewelry which might get caught in moving machinery.
4. Keep your hair cut short or wear a shop cap to keep long hair from getting caught in machinery.
5. Wear a shop coat or apron to protect your clothing.
6. Wear special protective clothing when working in foundry, forging, and welding.
7. Wear safety goggles or a face shield when drilling, grinding, buffing or when there is danger of flying chips.
8. Wear special goggles or shield when welding.

It has been said that a good mechanic seldom gets hurt. A good mechanic takes proper care of the tools he uses. Records show that most minor accidents are caused by incorrect use of hand tools, or the tools have not been kept in good repair. When you are working with tools in the metals area always follow these guides:

1. Do not use a tool until you have had a demonstration.
2. Report any defective or broken tool you find to the teacher.
3. Dull tools are dangerous and will not work properly. Keep all cutting edges sharp.
4. Check hammer handles to be sure they are not cracked, and are fastened tightly.
5. Never use a file without a handle.

Fig. 3-1. The cold chisel at the left has a mushroom head. The one at the right is properly ground.

6. Always grind mushroom heads and burrs off chisels, punches, and other hand tools, Fig. 3-1.
7. Never carry sharp tools in your pocket.
8. Always carry tools and projects so their points or sharp edges are pointing down. If this is impractical, protect sharp edges and points with heavy paper, pieces of wood, or a metal sheath.
9. Be sure your hands are dry when using portable electric hand tools. Do not stand in a wet spot, touch plumbing, or other grounded objects while using electrically powered tools.
10. Always ground portable electric hand tools. Check the electrical cord, connections, plug, and switch to be sure they are in good condition before using.
11. Do not use electrical tools around inflammable gases or vapors. This could cause an explosion.

To complete your safety program you will want to establish some good housekeeping guides. A clean and orderly shop provides a safe place to work. You will want to do your part in keeping the shop clean and in order. Clean the bench or machine after you have finished your work. Clean and put away all tools and accessories when you have finished using them. Wipe up any oil or grease which might have dropped on the floor. As you work in the shop you will discover other things you can do to make it a safer place to work. Always be alert for any situation that might cause an accident.

Remember these basic guides of safety and practice them:

1. Dress properly for the job.
2. Protect your eyes at all times.
3. Know your job and do it correctly.
4. Be a good housekeeper.
5. When in doubt check with your teacher.

QUIZ — UNIT 3

1. Describe the proper way to dress in the shop.
2. How are the eyes protected when:
   a. grinding?
   b. drilling?
   c. welding?
3. Why is the proper attitude an important factor in shop safety?
4. Why is it necessary to remove jewelry when working with moving machinery?
5. What kind of hand tools are most dangerous?
6. How should sharp tools be carried?
7. Why is it advisable to grind mushroom heads off chisels and punches?
8. List three safety precautions to be observed when using a portable electric drill.
9. Why is it dangerous to use electrical tools around inflammable gases or vapors?
10. Why is good housekeeping an important part of a shop safety program?

The sheet metal trades offer a variety of careers which start with the operation of production machines to the highly skilled craftsman who performs the operations with hand tools and machines.
(General Motors Corp.)

BENCH AND WROUGHT METAL

UNIT 4

1. How to use measuring and layout tools.
2. Cutting and drilling.
3. Bending and forming metal.
4. Cutting internal and external threads.
5. Fastening metals together.
6. Polishing and buffing metal.

Bench metal is basic to all areas of metalwork. It deals with the use of common hand tools and information necessary for all workers in the metal trades. In this area of metalwork you will learn to use hand tools for laying out, cutting, shaping, forming, drilling, threading, assembling, and testing work at the bench. You will be working with mild steel, aluminum, copper, etc. The metal will be in the form of rods, squares, flat bars, and sheet stock of various sizes and thicknesses. The metal is worked cold with hand tools and a few machines such as the drill press, grinder, and buffer. It is very important that you learn to use the hand tools which will be introduced in this unit because you will use many of them in other units of metalwork.

CAREER OPPORTUNITIES

Using hand tools correctly is often more difficult than operating some machines. A metalworker must be able to use hand tools skillfully. Aviation mechanics, auto mechanics, machine repairmen, and assemblers, to mention a few, offer excellent job opportunities to people who can use bench metal tools correctly.

Skilled bench metal workers must know how to read blueprints, engineering specifications, and use a variety of tools including precision measuring instruments. Some of the new fields that have appeared in the last few years, such as missile subassembly, work on instrumentation, and electronics components, require a very high degree of skill.

Learning to use hand tools will be very valuable to you regardless of how you earn your living. You will be able to take care of maintenance jobs around your home. Many have found bench-metal work to be a very interesting and satisfying hobby. It does not cost as much to equip a home work shop for bench-metal work as some other hobbies. You can make many useful items for your home and gifts for friends.

MEASURING AND LAYING OUT STOCK

The first steps in constructing a project are to measure your stock and mark it to the correct size, then transfer your patterns to the material being used. Making accurate measurements is very important in the production of high-grade work. To do this you will want to learn to use the following measuring and layout tools correctly.

RULES

The most widely used tool for taking and laying out measurements is the steel rule. Rules vary in lengths, widths, and thicknesses. The most common

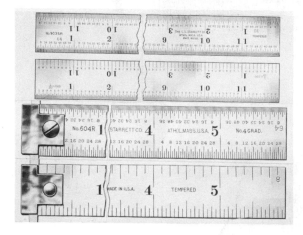

Fig. 4-1. Above. Two sides of a spring-tempered steel rule. Below. Two sides of an adjustable hook rule.
(L. S. Starrett Co.)

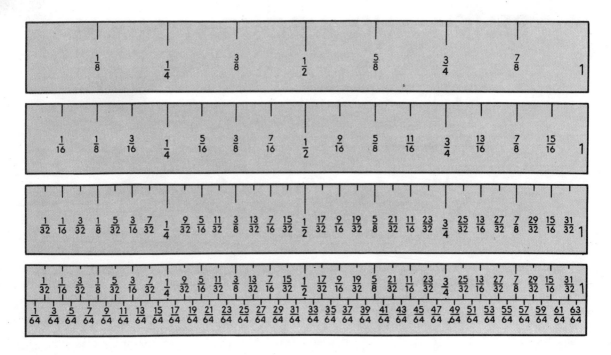

Fig. 4-2. Chart showing a comparison of the divisions on a rule.

being 6, 12, and 24 inches in length. Along each edge of the rule and on both sides, the inch marks are divided into various subdivisions. The first edge is divided into sixty-fourths of an inch. The second edge is divided into thirty-seconds of an inch and the third edge into sixteenths of an inch. The fourth edge, and the one you will use most is divided into eighths of an inch. Several types of steel rules with which you should become familiar are shown in Fig. 4-1.

Incorrect measurements in layout cause serious trouble in metalworking. Be sure you can read a rule. Study the chart shown in Fig. 4-2.

SCRIBER

A scriber is a pointed steel instrument which is used to scribe or scratch lines on most metal surfaces, Fig. 4-3. It is held in the same manner as a lead pencil, Fig. 4-4. Keep the point true and sharp.

SQUARES

The combination square set, with its four principal parts is a very useful measuring and layout tool, Fig. 4-5. The four parts are blade, combination square head, center head, and protractor head.

The blade which is available in lengths from 4 in. to 24 in. has graduations marked on all four edges.

Fig. 4-3. A scriber. (L. S. Starrett Co.)

Fig. 4-4. Hold the scriber like a pencil.

These graduations are usually 64ths, 32nds, 16ths, and 8ths. A groove runs along the center of the blade on one side and serves as a guide for clamping the heads. Each head can be slipped to any position along the length of the blade, and held in place with a knurled nut.

Fig. 4-5. Combination square set. A—Blade. B—45 and 90 deg. square head. C—Protractor head. D—Center head.

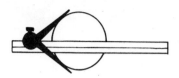

Fig. 4-7. Using the combination square center head.

The combination square head has a straight edge which forms a 90 deg. angle with the blade on one side, and a 45 deg. angle on the opposite side. This head, Fig. 4-6, has many uses.

The center head has two projecting arms which form an inside angle of 90 deg. This head is used to locate centers of round stock. To use it for this purpose, place the center head against the stock with the blade on the top surface, Fig. 4-7, and scribe a line along the blade edge. Move the tool around the stock, and scribe two or more lines approximately the same distance apart. The exact center of the stock will be at the intersection of these lines.

The protractor head has a straight edge with a revolving turret in the center. The revolving turret is divided into 180 degrees. It is used to lay out or check any angle from 0 to 180 degrees. To draw

angular lines, clamp blade to turret, set the blade at required degree, and lock in place with knurled nut. Then, place straight edge of head against edge of stock with blade across the surface, and scribe a line along the edge of the blade, Fig. 4-8.

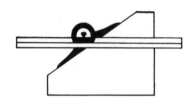

Fig. 4-8. Using the combination square protractor head.

Fig. 4-9. Dividers. (L.S. Starrett Co.)

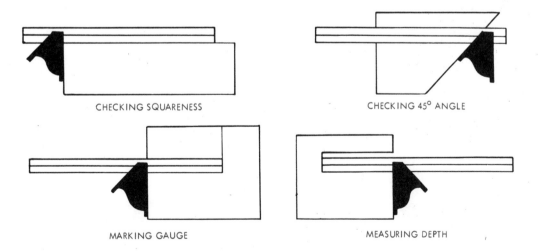

CHECKING SQUARENESS

CHECKING 45° ANGLE

MARKING GAUGE

MEASURING DEPTH

Fig. 4-6. Uses of the combination square head.

DIVIDERS

Dividers are used for measuring or setting off distances, and to lay out arcs and circles, Fig. 4-9. The procedure for using the dividers is the same as using a pencil compass in drawing.

PRICK PUNCH

The prick punch is a small center punch which is also known as a layout punch. Its point is ground at an angle of 30 degrees. It is used to accurately mark holes and other locations to be machined, Fig. 4-10. Keep the point true and sharp.

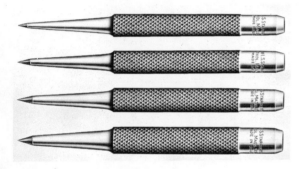

Fig. 4-10. A set of prick punches.

CENTER PUNCH

The center punch has one end ground to a 90 deg. conical point, Fig. 4-11. It is used to enlarge prick

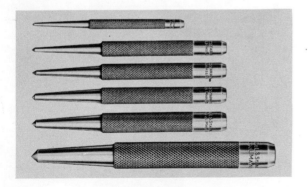

Fig. 4-11. A set of center punches.

punch marks and make it easier for the drill to start correctly. Keep the point true and sharp.

LAYING OUT STOCK

In laying out a job, an outline or pattern marked on the material shows the size and shape of the parts and the location of openings and holes. Laying out work varies, so the procedure given here may be changed to meet your particular situation. Remember when laying out stock for a project, accuracy is very important.

1. Check the end of the material from which the marking is being done to make sure it is square. Square the end if necessary.
2. Measure the stock for required length by placing a rule parallel to the edge of the stock. Check the end of the rule to be sure it is even with the square end of the stock. Make a short mark in line with the unit on the rule that represents the correct length, Fig. 4-12.

Fig. 4-12. Measuring length of stock. Mark length accurately with a scriber.

3. Mark a square line across stock at the correct length by placing a square over the stock, Fig. 4-13. The straight edge of the square head must be held firmly against the edge of the stock. Holding the scriber at a slight angle away from the blade of the square, and slanted slightly along the direction the line is to be drawn, mark a line across the stock. Cut off stock to length.
4. Prepare work for lay out of holes, cutouts, and irregular shapes by coating the surface with layout "bluing" fluid. This dries fast and provides a contrast between surface and scribed lines, Fig. 4-14.
5. Draw center lines across the length and width of the stock to serve as base lines from which all other layout lines can be accurately measured. If

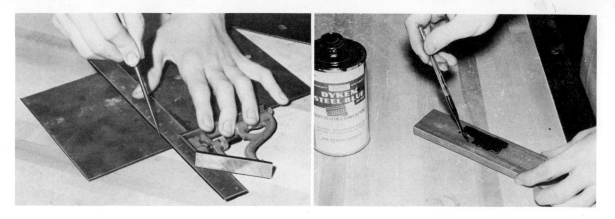

Fig. 4-13. Left. Marking a line across the stock with a combination square and a scriber. Fig. 4-14. Right. Applying layout fluid to piece of metal.

one edge of the material is even, it can be used as a base line.

6. Scribe all the straight lines first. Use center lines, or a true edge of the stock, to start all measurements.

7. Draw angular lines. Use the protractor head of the combination square set. It will be necessary to have one edge and one end true to be used as a base for the straight edge of the protractor head.

8. Draw irregular lines. Following are two methods which may be used:

   a. Use a template (pattern) of plywood or sheet metal. Place the template in place on the stock and trace around it with a scriber. This method is used when several pieces of the same shape are required.

   b. Transfer design to metal using carbon paper. Apply a coat of showcard white to metal. Place a piece of carbon paper and then the design over the metal. Trace the design with a pencil or blunt tool.

9. Scribe all arcs and circles on the metal with the dividers. To locate the center for an arc, measure in the distance required and square the lines which intersect at point A, Fig. 4-15. Make a small indentation with a prick punch where the two main lines intersect at A. Use a rule to set dividers for the required radius, Fig. 4-16. Insert

Fig. 4-16. Adjusting the dividers for a required radius.

Fig. 4-17. Using the dividers to scribe a circle.

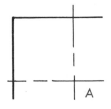

Fig. 4-15. Locating a center for laying out arcs and circles.

one point of the dividers in the center hole and, holding the stem by the thumb and forefinger, draw the arc or circle, Fig. 4-17.

19

10. Scribe lines on material to indicate all internal areas to be removed.

11. Lay out centers for holes. Locate all holes by measuring from two reference points and mark this area with two intersecting lines, Fig. 4-18. Make a small mark with a prick punch where these two lines intersect.

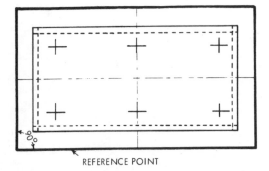

Fig. 4-18. Laying out location of holes to be drilled in stock.

CUTTING METAL

There are several tools and machines which can be used to cut ferrous and nonferrous metals. The most common tools are the hacksaw, cold chisel, bench shears, and power saw.

HACKSAWS

A hacksaw has a blade, a U-shaped frame, and a handle, Fig. 4-19.

Fig. 4-19. An adjustable type hacksaw frame.
(Stanley Tools)

BLADES

To get the best results from a hacksaw, it will be necessary for you to learn several facts about the different types of blades which are available so you can make a wise selection.

Size: Blades vary in length from 8 in. to 12 in., 1/2 in. wide and 0.025 in. thick for general duty work, 5/8 in. wide and 0.032 in. thick for heavy-duty work.

Material: Blades are made of high speed steel, tungsten alloy steel, molybdenum steel, and other special alloy steel.

Types: Only the teeth are hardened on a flexible-back blade. This type is considered best for the inexperienced worker, and makes a good all-around blade for general sawing. The all-hard type is hardened throughout the blade which makes them brittle and easy to break.

Fig. 4-20. Checking the number of teeth per inch.

Teeth: The number of teeth on a blade range from 14 to 32 teeth per inch, Fig. 4-20. Blades will last longer if you select one with the correct number of teeth for the job. Use a blade with 14 teeth for brass, aluminum, cast iron, and soft iron; 18 teeth for drill rod, mild steel, tool steel, and general work; 24 teeth for tubing, and pipe.

Set of teeth: This refers to the way the teeth are bent. This provides proper clearance for the blade which makes the cutting easier and faster, and it prevents overheating the blade. Fig. 4-21 shows four general types of saw sets. The wave set is used for fine-tooth blades.

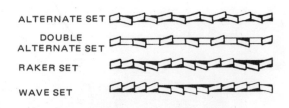

Fig. 4-21. Set of hacksaw blade teeth.

SAWING WITH HACKSAW

1. Select the correct blade, making sure that at least two teeth will be in contact with the metal at all times.
2. Fasten the blade in the frame <u>with the teeth pointing away from the handle</u>. Tighten the blade with enough tension to hold it rigidly between the pins.
3. Secure the stock in a vise, or with clamps. The line where you are going to make the cut should be close to the end of the vise jaw or clamp, Fig. 4-22.

RIGHT   WRONG

Fig. 4-23. Correct blade angle for starting cuts.

Fig. 4-22. Clamp stock tightly in vise. The line where the cut is to be made should be close to the vise jaws.

4. Hold the saw at the correct angle. Fig. 4-23 shows the right and wrong angles for cutting.
5. Start the cut with a light, steady forward stroke. At the end of each stroke, relieve the pressure and draw the blade <u>straight back</u>. After two or three strokes to get the cut started, take full-length strokes in a straight line. Do not allow saw to wobble. Hold the saw firmly with both hands. Continue sawing, using long steady strokes at a pace of 40 to 50 strokes per minute. Use just enough pressure on the forward stroke to make each tooth remove a small amount of metal, Fig. 4-24. Remember--<u>do not use any pressure on the back stroke</u>. Do not allow the teeth to drag over the metal.
6. Slow down near the end of the cut so you can control the saw when stock is sawed through.

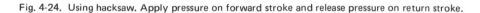

Fig. 4-24. Using hacksaw. Apply pressure on forward stroke and release pressure on return stroke.

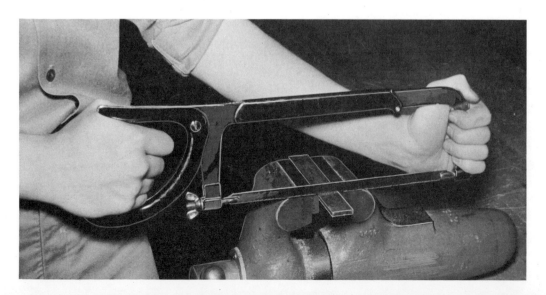

7. To make a long cut along the side of a piece of metal, turn the blade at right angles to the frame. This makes it possible to saw a cut deeper than the saw frame would otherwise allow.

CHISELS

A chisel is a wedge-shaped tool used to shear, cut, and chip metal. When you cannot use tin snips or a hacksaw for cutting, reach for a chisel. It is your metal-cutting troubleshooter. It can be used in hard-to-get-to places for such jobs as shearing off rivets, smoothing castings, or splitting rusted nuts from bolts. A chisel will cut any metal that is softer than its own cutting edge, which is hardened and sharpened. There are four principal kinds of chisels used in bench metal work, Fig. 4-25.

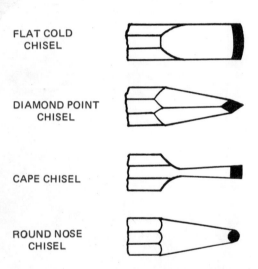

FLAT COLD CHISEL

DIAMOND POINT CHISEL

CAPE CHISEL

ROUND NOSE CHISEL

Fig. 4-25. Four kinds of chisels commonly used in metalwork.

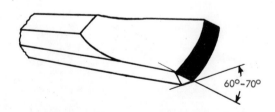

Fig. 4-26. The correct shape and point angle of a cold chisel.

1. Flat cold chisel — used for cutting, shearing, and chipping. The size is determined by the width of the cutting edge.
2. Cape chisel — used for cutting keyways, square corners or slots.

3. Diamond point chisel — used for cutting V-grooves and inside sharp angles.
4. Round nose chisel — used to cut rounded or semi-circular grooves, corners which have fillets, and to "draw back" a drill which has "walked away" from its intended center.

You will use the flat cold chisel for most of your work. Keep your chisel sharp and ground at an angle of 60 to 70 deg. and the edge at a slight arc, Fig. 4-26. When grinding a chisel, hold it against the wheel with very little pressure to avoid overheating. Dip the point in water often to keep it cool. If the point heats it will "draw" the temper of the steel. If this happens, the cutting edge will become soft and useless until it is rehardened and tempered.

Blows of the hammer will cause the head of the chisel to spread at the top like a mushroom. This is dangerous because chunks of metal will break away from the overhanging mushroom with enough force to cause an injury. Always keep the head ground as in B, Fig. 4-27.

Fig. 4-27. Always keep the head of chisels ground like "B."

CUTTING METAL WITH A COLD CHISEL

Following are two methods used to cut metal with a flat cold chisel:

A. Cutting over flat plate.
1. Scribe outline of pattern on metal.
2. Place metal on top of a lead or soft steel back plate. Do not use finished surface of anvil, or vise.
3. Grasp chisel in one hand, Fig. 4-28. Hold chisel in a perpendicular position with the cutting edge on the line to be cut.
4. Strike the head of the chisel lightly with a ball-peen hammer. Keep your eyes focused on the line to be cut, not on the chisel. Move the chisel for the next cut. Check after each

Fig. 4-28. Cutting metal with a chisel.

blow of the hammer to be sure the cutting edge of the chisel is on the outline to be cut.

5. Continue the light cut until you have cut around the outline.
6. Place the chisel at the starting point and cut around the outline again. Use heavier blows this time.
7. Continue cutting around outline until chisel is nearly through metal. Use lighter blows to finish cutting and to prevent cutting into the back plate.

B. Shearing in a vise.

1. Clamp the metal securely in the vise with the line to be cut slightly above the top edge of the vise jaw.
2. Place the beveled surface of the chisel's cutting edge flat on the vise jaw, Fig. 4-29.

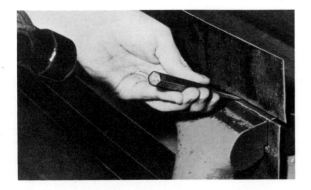

Fig. 4-29. Shearing metal.

The chisel will have a tendency to dig in if held too high. It will tear the metal and you will not get the proper cutting action if it is held too low.

3. Holding the chisel firmly and at an angle toward the work, direct the center of the cutting edge at the line to be cut so you will get a shearing action.
4. Start cutting at one end of the metal and strike the chisel hard enough to cut through the material. After each cut, advance the chisel until shearing is completed.

FILES

A file is a hard steel instrument made in various sizes, shapes, and cuts of teeth. Files are used for cutting, smoothing, and removing small amounts of metal. Fig. 4-30 shows the parts of a file. The three distinguishing features of files are length, kind, and cut.

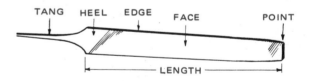

Fig. 4-30. Parts of a file.

Length: The length of the file is the distance between the heel and the point. The tang which is made to hold the handle is not included in the length.

Kind (or name): This means the various shapes or styles which are called by such names as flat, mill, half-round, etc. These are divided according to the form of their cross-sections into three general geometrical classes — quadrangular (four-sided), circular, and triangular.

The cut: This refers to the character of the teeth; such as single, double, rasp, and curved, Fig. 4-31,

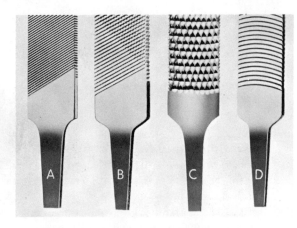

Fig. 4-31. Cuts of files: (A) Single cut; (B) Double cut; (C) Rasp cut; (D) Curved-tooth cut. (Nicholson File Co.)

Fig. 4-32. Machinists' files: (A) Mill file; single cut, used for draw filing and finishing; (B) Flat file; double cut, for general work; (C) Half round file; double cut, used to file curved surfaces; (D) Hand bastard file; double cut, for finishing flat surfaces--it also has one safe edge (without teeth).

and also to the coarseness of the teeth; rough, coarse, bastard, second cut, smooth and dead smooth. Some machinists' files used in the metal shop are shown in Fig. 4-32.

Selecting the correct file for the work to be done is very important, in order to obtain the greatest efficiency in filing. Many factors enter into the selection of the right file for the job.

1. Size of work: Use a large file on large work and a small file for small work.
2. Flat or convex surface: Use a flat-shaped file for flat surfaces and a half-round or round-shaped file for curved surfaces.
3. Rough cutting: Use a coarse, double-cut file.
4. Square corners and enlarging square or rectangular openings: Use a square file.
5. Filing circular openings or curved surfaces: Use a round file.
6. Finishing a surface: Use a single-cut file in the second cut bastard, or a smooth file.
7. Hard steels: Use a second-cut file.
8. Soft steels: Use a bastard file.
9. Brass, aluminum, and lead: Use a special file, Fig. 4-31d.
10. Draw filing: Use a single-cut mill file.

FILING METAL

Filing is an art. The grip, pressure, and stroke must vary to fit the work being done and the kind of file used. Following are two methods for filing that you will use in bench metal work:

Straight filing. This method consists of pushing the file lengthwise--straight ahead or slightly diagonally--across the work.

1. Fasten the stock to be filed securely in a vise. The surface to be filed should be parallel to the vise jaws and a short distance above them to prevent "chattering" (excessive vibration).
2. Select the correct file for the job. For light and accurate filing, grasp the handle with one hand, allowing its end to fit into and up against the fleshy part of the palm below the joint of the little finger, with the thumb lying parallel along the top of the handle and the fingers pointing upward. Grasp the point of the file by the thumb and the first two fingers of the other hand, Fig. 4-33. For heavy work grasp the handle in the same manner just described. Place the palm of the hand on top of the point of the file with the fingers curled under, Fig. 4-34.
3. File the metal by "carrying" (stroke) the file forward on an almost straight line--changing its course often enough to prevent "grooving." A file cuts only on the forward stroke--release the pressure on the back stroke. Use a uniform stroking motion and keep the file flat on the work. Do not allow the file to "rock" as this will produce a rounded surface. Various metals require different touches, but in general, apply just enough pressure on the forward stroke to keep the file cutting at all times. If allowed to slide over hard metals the teeth will become dull.
4. Clean the file. The teeth become clogged with particles of metal. To do a good job of filing, these filings or "chips" which collect between the teeth must be removed to keep the file working efficiently and prevent the "chips" from scratching

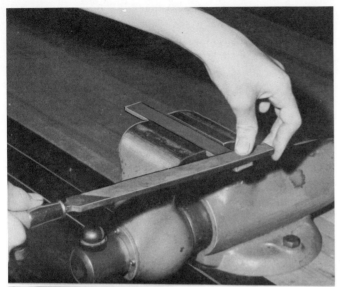

Fig. 4-35. Cleaning a file with a file card. Brush with the angle at which the teeth are cut.

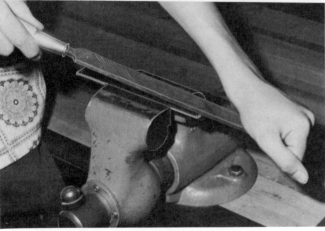

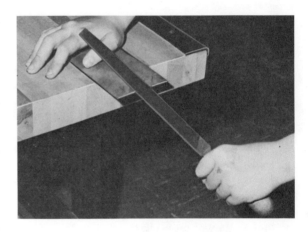

Fig. 4-36. Removing burrs from the edge of metal.

Fig. 4-33. Above. The proper way to hold a file for light filing. Fig. 4-34. Below. The proper way to hold a file for heavy filing.

your work. The teeth should be brushed frequently with a file card or brush, Fig. 4-35. Never strike your file against the bench or vise to clean it--the teeth are brittle and easily broken. When taking very fine cuts or in filing soft metals, such as copper and brass, rub the face of the file with chalk to prevent the teeth from becoming clogged.

5. Check the surfaces being filed for squareness. Hold the work up to the light and place a rule or square on the surface. If light shows between the surface being checked and the square, mark the high spots. File the high spots lightly and check again. Continue this procedure until the stock is square.

6. Remove burrs from edges. When cutting or filing heavy sheet stock, burrs form on the edges.

Remove these burrs by running the file across the sharp edges, Fig. 4-36.

Draw filing. This operation is performed by grasping the file at each end and pushing and drawing it across the work. A very smooth surface can be obtained by this method. Generally a mill bastard file is used for draw filing.

1. Grasp the file firmly at each end and place the file on the work at the end away from you.
2. Holding the file steady, apply sufficient pressure to get a cutting action, and draw file toward you, Fig. 4-37. At the end of each stroke lift the file and return to the starting point. Use a new section of the file for each stroke. After one side of the file has been used up turn it over and use the other side. After both sides have been used, clean the file before continuing. This is important. A chip between the teeth will scratch the filled surface.

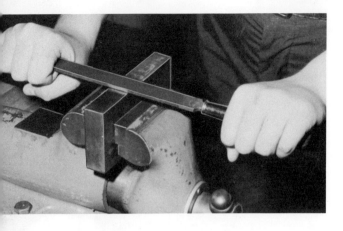

Fig. 4-37. Draw filing.

Protect your files by observing these rules:

1. Always keep a good handle on your file. The tang has a sharp point which can pierce your hand. Never use a file without a handle.
2. Never use a new file to remove scale from metal. Use an old, worn file for this job.
3. Avoid getting files oily. Oil causes a file to slide across the work and prevents fast, clean cutting.
4. Protect the file teeth. Always hang files in a rack when not in use. Never allow the teeth to come in contact with other files or tools. If you put a file in a toolbox or drawer with other tools, wrap the file with cloth.
5. Keep the file clean. Use a file card to clean the file after every few strokes. Sometimes it is necessary to use a sharp pointed nail or piece of wire to remove stubborn "chips."
6. Never use a file for prying or pounding. The body of a file is hard and very brittle. A slight bend or a

fall to the floor might break the file.

7. Never hammer on a file. Since it is hard and extremely brittle the blows might cause sharp chips to fly in all directions and injure someone.

CUTTING HOLES IN METAL

One way to produce holes in solid metal is to use a drill. Holes up to 1/2 in. in diameter can be drilled by hand with a hand or breast drill, Fig. 4-38. A portable electric drill is also a very useful and fast tool for drilling holes in metal. When drilling holes larger than 1/2 in. in diameter use a drill press, Fig. 4-39.

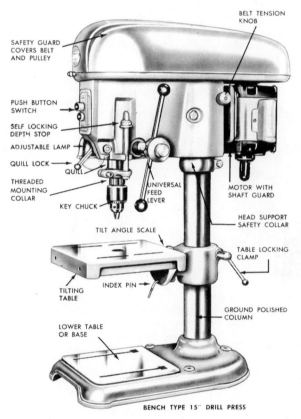

Fig. 4-39. A drill press.

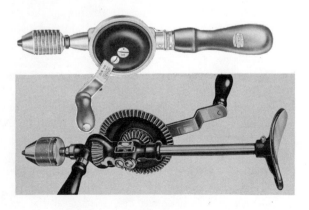

Fig. 4-38. Above. Hand drill. Below. Breast drill.
(Stanley Tools)

The actual cutting of holes is done with a twist drill. A drill has three main parts, the shank, the body, and the point, Fig. 4-40. The shank end fits into the chuck or spindle of the drilling machine. The most commonly used twist drills are made of carbon steel and high speed alloy steel. The two types of shanks most commonly used are the straight and taper, Fig. 4-41. The body of the drill is the section

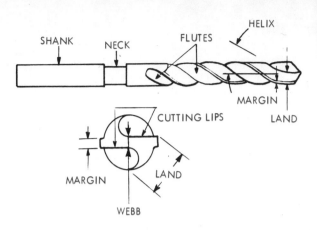

Fig. 4-40. The parts of a twist drill.

Fig. 4-42. Checking the size of a drill with a drill gauge.

Fig. 4-41. Two types of drill shanks. Above. Straight shank. Below. Taper shank.   (Cleveland Twist Drill Co.)

extending from the shank to the point. The two spiral grooves running around the body are called flutes. The point of the drill which does the cutting is the "business end" of the drill. The point is formed by the ends of the web, flutes, and margins of the drill body. The two sharp edges that do the cutting are called lips. The lips must be sharp and properly ground to do an efficient job of cutting.

The twist drills you will use most frequently are those made in fractional sizes which start at 1/64 in. and go to 1 in. in diameter. The size is stamped on the shank of the drill. If the size number has worn off the drill shank, you can check the size with a Drill Gauge, Fig. 4-42. Because these drills vary 1/64 in. from one size to the next, two other systems have been developed to provide in between sizes. Number drills range from No. 80 to No. 1, and letter drills range from A to Z. Fig. 4-43, shows these drill sizes and their decimal equivalent.

There are five things that must be checked when grinding a drill:

1. Lip angle. For most work the two lips should form an angle of 59 deg., Fig. 4-44.
2. Lip length. Both cutting edges (lips) must be the same length, Fig. 4-44. If the lips are of unequal length the drill will cut oversize.

Number Drills	Fractional Drills	Decimal Equiv.	Number Drills	Letter Drills	Fractional Drills	Decimal Equiv.	Letter Drills	Fractional Drills	Decimal Equiv.
80		.0135			1/8	.1250	O		.3160
79		.0145	30			.1285	P		.3230
	1/64	.0156	29			.1360		21/64	.3281
78		.0160	28			.1405	Q		.3320
77		.0180			9/64	.1406	R		.3390
76		.0200	27			.1440		11/32	.3437
75		.0210	26			.1470	S		.3480
74		.0225	25			.1495	T		.3580
73		.0240	24			.1520		23/64	.3594
72		.0250	23			.1540	U		.3680
71		.0260			5/32	.1562		3/8	.3750
70		.0280	22			.1570	V		.3770
69		.0292	21			.1590	W		.3860
68		.0310	20			.1610		25/64	.3906
	1/32	.0312	19			.1660	X		.3970
67		.0320	18			.1695	Y		.4040
66		.0330			11/64	.1719		13/32	.4062
65		.0350	17			.1720	Z		.4130
64		.0360	16			.1770		27/64	.4219
63		.0370	15			.1800		7/16	.4375
62		.0380	14			.1820		29/64	.4531
61		.0390	13			.1850		15/32	.4687
60		.0400			3/16	.1875		31/64	.4844
59		.0410	12			.1890		1/2	.5000
58		.0420	11			.1910		33/64	.5156
57		.0430	10			.1935		17/32	.5312
56		.0465	9			.1960		35/64	.5469
	3/64	.0469	8			.1990		9/16	.5625
55		.0520	7			.2010		37/64	.5781
54		.0550			13/64	.2031		19/32	.5937
53		.0595	6			.2040		39/64	.6094
	1/16	.0625	5			.2055		5/8	.6250
52		.0635	4			.2090		41/64	.6406
51		.0670	3			.2130		21/32	.6562
50		.0700			7/32	.2187		43/64	.6719
49		.0730	2			.2210		11/16	.6875
48		.0760	1			.2280		45/64	.7031
	5/64	.0781		A		.2340		23/32	.7187
47		.0785			15/64	.2344		47/64	.7344
46		.0810		B		.2380		3/4	.7500
45		.0820		C		.2420		49/64	.7656
44		.0860		D		.2460		25/32	.7812
43		.0890		E	1/4	.2500		51/64	.7969
42		.0935		F		.2570		13/16	.8125
	3/32	.0937		G		.2610		53/64	.8281
41		.0960			17/64	.2656		27/32	.8437
40		.0980		H		.2660		55/64	.8594
39		.0995		I		.2720		7/8	.8750
38		.1015		J		.2770		57/64	.8906
37		.1040		K		.2810		29/32	.9062
36		.1065			9/32	.2812		59/64	.9219
	7/64	.1094		L		.2900		15/16	.9375
35		.1100		M		.2950		61/64	.9531
34		.1110			19/64	.2969		31/32	.9687
33		.1130		N		.3020		63/64	.9844
32		.1160			5/16	.3125		1	1.0000
31		.1200							

Fig. 4-43. Drill sizes and their decimal equivalents.

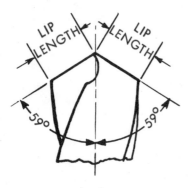

Fig. 4-44. Correctly ground drill lips.

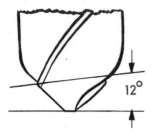

Fig. 4-45. Angle of lip clearance.

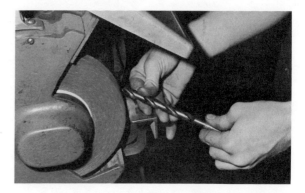

Fig. 4-46. The correct way to hold a drill for grinding.

3. Lip clearance. Only the cutting edge of the two lips should contact the metal being drilled. The surface behind the cutting edge of each lip must be ground back at an angle of 12 deg. to provide proper clearance, Fig. 4-45. This angle can be increased to 15 deg. for heavy feeds in soft metals.
4. Lip sharpness. The drill will not cut properly if the lips are rounded and dull, or chipped and burned.
5. Full margin. The distance from margin-to-margin determines the diameter of the drill. If the margin is worn away or broken, the drill will heat excessively and cut a tapered, undersize hole.

PROCEDURE FOR GRINDING A DRILL

Note: Practice the first two steps without turning on the grinder to get the "feel" of the angles and movements required to grind the drill properly:

1. Hold the drill near the point with your forefinger and thumb of one hand. Cradle the drill in the first joint of your forefinger and place the back of your finger on the tool rest. Grasp the drill shank with the thumb and forefinger of your other hand. Keep the drill shank to the left, and move the point forward so that one lip comes in contact with the grinding wheel, Fig. 4-46.

2. Keep the shank slightly lower than the point. As the lip contacts the wheel, push down on the drill shank so that the heel (back of the lip) of the drill is moved along the grinding wheel face. When the back edge of the heel surface is reached, the drill should be pulled away from the grinding wheel.
3. After you have practiced steps 1 and 2 a few times, turn on the grinder switch. Start grinding the drill, removing very little metal at first. Try to maintain the original shape of the point. Move the drill steadily and evenly, maintaining uniform pressure against the wheel as you grind. Check your work frequently with a drill-point gauge to be sure that you have the proper lip clearance of 12 deg., the proper lip angle of 59 deg., and that the two lips are the same length, Fig. 4-47. Do not allow the drill to overheat while sharpening. Drills can be cooled in water. Cool high-speed drills in the air otherwise they might crack.

DRILLING BY HAND

The hand drill is used to drill holes 1/4 inch in diameter or smaller. Its "big brother," the breast drill, is designed for tougher jobs and will drill holes up to 1/2 inch in diameter. Following is the procedure for using hand and breast drills:

1. Center punch hole locations as indicated by the prick punch marks which were made during the layout operation, Fig. 4-48. Make the opening with the center punch large enough to receive the point of the drill.
2. Select the correct size drill. To insert drill in the chuck, grip the crank handle and body of the hand drill tightly with one hand. Use the other hand to turn the chuck shell to open the jaws wide enough to allow the drill shank you are going to use to

Fig. 4-47. Checking the point with a drill grinding gauge.

Fig. 4-48. Using a center punch.

enter. Tighten the jaws of the chuck so the drill is held firmly.

3. Secure material to be drilled in a vise or clamp it to a bench. If possible, clamp piece in a position so drilling can be done horizontally. Place the point

Fig. 4-49. A portable electric hand drill.
(Stanley Tools)

of the drill in the center punch opening and crank drill at a moderate speed, making sure that you hold it at the proper angle with the work, usually 90 deg. Hold the drill steady, and apply enough pressure to keep the point cutting.

4. When the drill point is about to break through the metal, ease up on the pressure. Should the drill catch or jam in the material, finish cutting the hole by turning the chuck by hand. The drill should not be allowed to project through the hole any farther than is necessary to complete the hole. When the hole is completed, remove the drill. Continue to turn the drill in a clockwise direction and pull back on the handle.

DRILLING WITH PORTABLE POWER DRILL

The portable electric drill, Fig. 4-49, is used the same way as a hand drill, except that you do not have to crank it. Portable electric drills vary in size. The two most common sizes have a rated capacity of 1/4 in. and 1/2 in. in steel. To drill holes with a portable electric drill:

1. Place work in a vise or clamp it to the bench. The drilling can be done either horizontally or vertically.
2. Insert proper size drill bit for the job into drill chuck. Tighten the jaws against the drill bit with the chuck key.
3. With the power off, place the point of the drill in the center punch opening.
4. Hold the drill with one hand and steady it with the other. Turn on the power and apply steady pressure, Fig. 4-50.
5. When the drill point is about to break through the material, ease up on the pressure. Remove the drill from the hole and turn off the power. Do not allow the drill bit to jerk or bind since this will probably cause it to break off.

DRILLING WITH A DRILL PRESS

The drill press automatically holds and rotates the drill bit at the proper angle with the work. Drill presses vary in sizes ranging from small bench models to huge multiple-spindle types. When you use a drill press follow this procedure:

1. Locate the center of the hole to be drilled and mark the hole with a prick punch.
2. Enlarge the hole with a center punch.

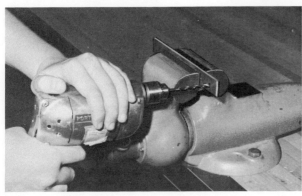

Fig. 4-50. Left. Using an electric hand drill. Fig. 4-51. Right. Inserting a drill in the drill press chuck.

3. Select the correct size drill and insert the drill in the chuck. Tighten the drill with the chuck key, Fig. 4-51.

4. Clamp the work to the table of the drill press. The type of clamp or jig used will depend on the nature of the job. Adjust the work so the point of the drill is lined up with the center mark. Place the drill press table at the correct height for the job. Check to see that the drill bit will pass through a clearance hole or slot in the table and there is no danger of drilling into the table. Fig. 4-52 shows several ways to hold metal while it is being drilled.

5. Adjust the drill press for the correct speed. The speed for drilling holes varies with the size of drill bit and material being used. The larger the drill bit, the slower the speed. A slow speed is used for hard metals and a higher speed for soft metals.

6. Turn on the power and bring the drill point down to the piece slowly. Feed the drill into the center mark with a steady, even pressure. Apply cutting fluid often enough during drilling operation to keep the drill bit lubricated and from becoming too hot.

7. Reduce the pressure slightly when the drill bit begins to go through the bottom side of the piece. This will help prevent the drill from catching.

8. When drilling holes larger than 3/8 in. it is good practice to drill a small pilot hole first. The diameter of the pilot hole, which is sometimes called a lead hole, should be approximately the size of the web thickness of the larger drill.

9. Holes which are to receive tapered heads of rivets, screws or bolts, must be countersunk. This may be done with a countersink drill, Fig. 4-53, or by using a drill bit twice the diameter of the hole.

Fig. 4-53. A countersink drill.
(Cleveland Twist Drill Co.)

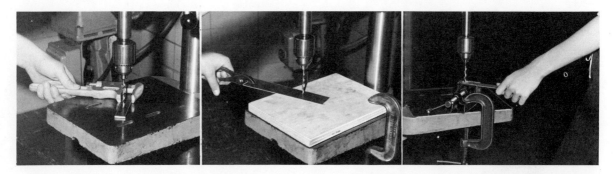

Fig. 4-52. Holding work while drilling. Left. Holding work with a monkey wrench. Center. Using a pair of pliers to hold thin stock. Right. Pieces clamped in drill press vise.

Countersink the hole enough to allow the head of the rivet, screw, or bolt to fit flush with the surface of the metal, Fig. 4-54.

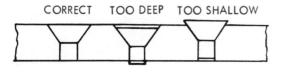

Fig. 4-54. Correct and incorrect way to countersink a hole.

BENDING, FORMING, AND TWISTING METAL

Some of your projects will require the bending of metal at right angles, acute angles, and obtuse angles. Other pieces of your project may require scroll work or the twisting of some of the parts. Most of the ferrous and nonferrous metals 1/4 in. or less in thickness can be bent cold. To make angular bends follow this procedure:

1. Make a full-size layout of the part to be bent, so you can determine the amount of metal to allow for the bends. To make a right-angle bend, add an amount equal to one-half the thickness of the metal for each bend. For example, if you are using 1/8 in. thick material, and you are going to make two right-angle bends, add 1/8 in. to the length of material, Fig. 4-55.

2. When more than one bend is to be made, decide on the order of bending so you can determine where to make the allowances for bending in the layout. This is necessary because the extra amount

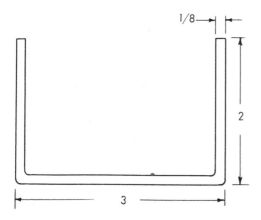

Fig. 4-55. Allow one-half the thickness of the metal for each bend.

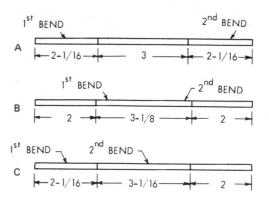

Fig. 4-56. Allowances laid out for the order of bending. The allowance has been added to the section that is to undergo the actual bending.

added to the length of the material for bending should always be placed above the vise jaws when making the bend, Fig. 4-56.

3. Clamp the metal in the vise with the bend line at

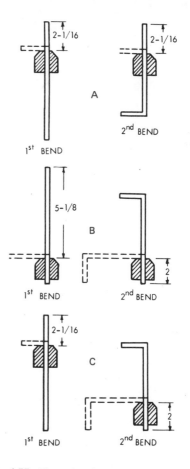

Fig. 4-57. The order of bending layouts which are shown in (A), (B), and (C), Fig. 4-56.

the top of the jaws, with the allowance end above the jaws, Fig. 4-57. Check the material with a square to make sure it is straight.

4. Bend the metal by applying pressure with one hand, and striking the metal near the jaws of the vise with a hammer at the same time, Fig. 4-58. Strike the metal just hard enough to complete the bend.

5. Check the bend with a square to make sure the bend is accurate.

6. To make a bend that is greater than 90 degrees (obtuse angle) use a monkey wrench, Fig. 4-59. It

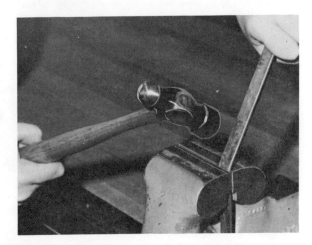

Fig. 4-58. Bending metal in a vise.

Fig. 4-59. Making a bend that is greater than 90 deg.

is not necessary to make any allowance for very shallow bends. If the bend is close to a right angle, an allowance should be made.

7. To make a bend that is less than 90 degrees (acute angle) the same allowance as made for a right angle bend must be made. Follow the procedure for making a right angle bend. To obtain the sharp

angle, place the right angle bend between the jaws of the vise, and squeeze the two sides together until the correct angle is obtained, Fig. 4-60.

Fig. 4-60. Making a bend that is less than 90 deg.

BENDING CURVES

Many projects require circular bends. This type of bending can be done by forming the metal around a rod or pipe, or with bending and forming machines. Most metal 1/4 in. or less can be formed cold.

To form circular bends, clamp a rod or piece of pipe in a vise. Place the metal over this piece, in the vise. Strike the metal glancing blows with a ball-peen hammer, Fig. 4-61. Move the metal forward gradually, striking the metal until the desired curve is formed.

Another method that may be used when a certain radius or diameter circle is to be formed is to clamp a piece of pipe or rod equal to the inside diameter of the circle or radius in a vise, with the piece of stock to be bent clamped between the rod or pipe and the solid jaw of the vise, Fig. 4-62. Grasp the end of the stock extending above the vise jaws, and pull the metal down against the bending device. Loosen the vise jaws and feed the stock in around the rod, and clamp in place as before. Continue this procedure until the desired circle or radius has been formed. Metal that is too thick to be formed by hand can be bent around the bending device by pulling it with one

Fig. 4-61. Forming a circular bend over a rod.

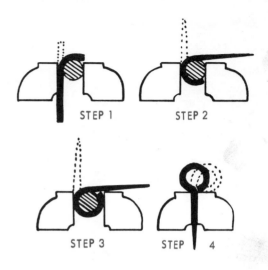

Fig. 4-63. Steps in forming an eye.

Fig. 4-62. Fasten both the rod and the work in the vise. Draw the work around the rod.

hand and striking it close to the bending device with a ball-peen hammer. Continue the bending operation by feeding the metal around the bending device and hammering it down against the bending device until the desired circle or radius is obtained.

A small eye can be formed by clamping the stock to be bent, and a piece of cylindrical pipe or rod equal to the inside diameter of the eye, in a vise. Follow the steps shown in Fig. 4-63.

TWISTING METAL

Very interesting and pleasing lines can be added to parts of a metal project by twisting some of the pieces. Twisting is also used to give additional strength and to change the position of the piece so it can be fastened at the ends. Mild steel band iron 1/4 in. or less in thickness and 1 1/2 in. or less in width, can be bent cold. Square rods of mild steel up to 1/2 in. can be bent without heating. To bend larger sizes of stock, heat the metal to a dull red color in a forge or with a torch.

The procedure for twisting metal is:

1. Determine the portion of the stock to be twisted, and the number of desired twists. Calculate the amount of stock to allow for twisting (which tends to shorten stock) by taking a scrap piece of metal the same kind to be twisted and check the length. Make a single twist in this test piece and check the length. The difference between the length before, and after twisting, is the amount to allow for each twist to be made.

2. Mark off the section of the metal to be twisted. If duplicate pieces are to be made, mark them at the same time.

3. Place the metal to be twisted in a vise with one of the limit marks for the section to be twisted even with the outer edge of the vise jaw. Short pieces should be clamped in a vertical position, and long pieces should be clamped in a horizontal position. Clamp a monkey wrench at the other end of the section to be twisted, Fig. 4-64. The twist may be

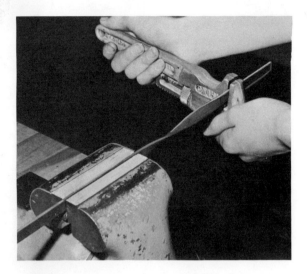

Fig. 4-64. Twisting metal with a wrench.

made to the right or left. Rotate the wrench until the desired number of twists have been obtained.

4. When twisting a long piece of metal, it is sometimes difficult to keep it straight. This can be corrected to some extent by slipping a piece of pipe which is slightly larger than the metal, over the section to be twisted.

5. If the piece of metal needs straightening after being twisted, place it over a hardwood block and hammer it with a wood or lead mallet, Fig. 4-65.

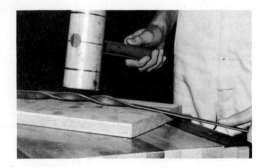

Fig. 4-65. Straightening metal after twisting.

Do not strike the metal hard enough to damage the twist. Rotate the metal as you straighten it so the portion not touching the surface of the board can be brought in line with the surface of the board. Continue this procedure until the metal is straight.

FORMING A SCROLL

A scroll is a piece of metal which has been bent to a circular shape to form a spiral similar to the shape that would be formed if a clock spring were spread open, Fig. 4-66. Scroll work is used mainly for

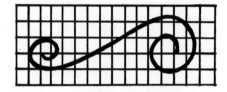

Fig. 4-66. A scroll.

decorative purposes. When properly used, scrolls break up the monotony of straight lines and add interesting features to projects. Scrolls may be formed by using jigs, forks, and other devices.

The procedure for forming a scroll is:

1. Lay out a full-size pattern of the desired scroll on a piece of heavy wrapping paper or cardboard. This pattern is used to help determine the length of stock needed and to check the work as the bending proceeds.

2. Determine the length of stock that will be needed for the scroll by forming a piece of soft wire or stock on the pattern. Then straighten the wire and measure its length.

3. Cut the stock to the correct length. Decorate the surface and the ends of the stock as desired. See Figs. 4-74 and 4-75. Select the bending device and clamp it in a vise or to a bench, Fig. 4-67.

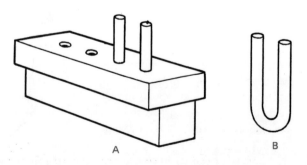

Fig. 4-67. Scroll bending devices. Left. Metal block with pins that can be adjusted for different thicknesses of metal. Right. U-shaped bending fork made from a rod.

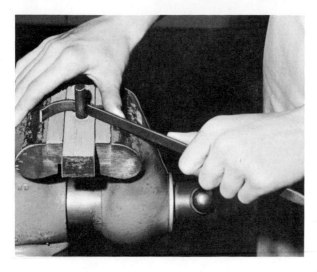

Fig. 4-68. Forming a scroll by hand.

4. Start forming the scroll by grasping the end of the metal with one hand, placing the other end in the bending device and holding it in place with the other hand, Fig. 4-68. Apply pressure with the thumb of the hand at the bending jig. Use the other hand to pull the metal against the bending jig with enough pressure to start forming the scroll. Move the metal into the jig a little at a time and continue to apply even pressure. This allows the scroll to form evenly and gradually without sharp bends. Most beginners have trouble forming scrolls without sharp bends because they try to

form too much between each application of pressure. By developing a rhythm of sliding the metal through the jig (not over 1/8 in. at a time) and applying pressure to the metal at the jig each time the metal is moved forward, smooth curves can be produced without kinks. Form a small section of the scroll and check it by placing the piece on the full-size pattern, Fig. 4-69. Complete this section of the scroll to be formed. If the curve of the scroll needs to be corrected, it can be opened by placing the metal back in the jig and applying pressure in the opposite direction. Be sure to do this gradually, moving metal through the jig a little at a time. Continue to form the metal and check often until the scroll fits the pattern.

5. When the scroll has been completely formed, check it to see if it will lie flat. If the scroll needs to be straightened, place it in a vise edgewise and straighten it by hand, Fig. 4-70.

Fig. 4-70. Straightening scroll so it will lie flat.

BENDING SMALL PIPE AND TUBING

Pipe and tubing can be formed successfully by using a jig, Fig. 4-71. If a sharp bend is necessary, fill the pipe or tubing with wet sand or molten lead. This will prevent the pipe or tubing from collapsing while being formed. Place the pipe or tubing on the jig and slowly draw it around the form. Remove the sand or lead after the desired shape has been formed.

Fig. 4-69. Checking scroll on a full-size pattern.

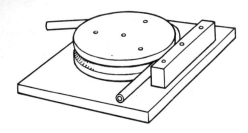

Fig. 4-71. Jig for bending pipe and tubing.

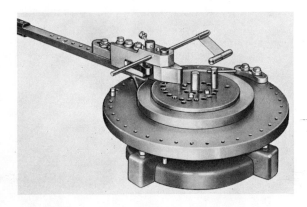

Fig. 4-72. A No. 2 Di-Acro bending machine.
(Irwin O'Neil Mfg. Co.)

BENDING AND FORMING MACHINES

There are several machines available for bending and forming metal accurately and smoothly. Fig. 4-72 shows a No. 2 Di-Acro bending machine which can be used to form flats, rods, tubing, channel, and angle. Fig. 4-73 shows the bender being used to make various bends.

SAMMY SAFETY
SAYS:

"When filling a pipe or piece of tubing with molten lead, be sure it is completely dry. Moisture causes molten metal to splatter and it might cause a serious accident."

DECORATING ENDS OF METAL

The ends of band iron can be made attractive and their appearance improved by grinding, filing, cutting, or hammering. Some possible shapes are shown in Fig. 4-74. To make a shape like (b), first lay out the

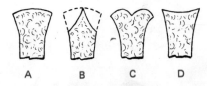

Fig. 4-74. Suggested end designs for band iron. (A) Fan shaped; (B) Arrow head; (C) Fish tail; (D) Flared.

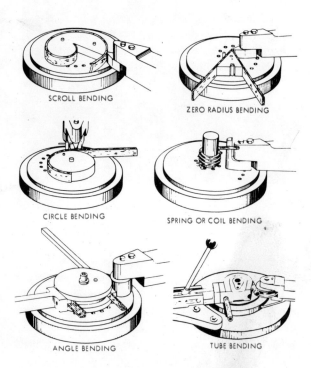

SCROLL BENDING

ZERO RADIUS BENDING

CIRCLE BENDING

SPRING OR COIL BENDING

ANGLE BENDING

TUBE BENDING

Fig. 4-73. Some bends that can be made on Di-Acro bending machine.

design on the end of the metal. Spread the end of metal into a fan shape (indicated by dotted lines) by placing the end of the metal near the edge of an anvil and by striking the metal with a ball-peen hammer. Continue striking the end of the metal, working from edge to edge with closely spaced blows until the end takes a fan shape. Grind the end to a pointed shape. Finish the ground edges of the metal by hammering them down to a thin edge so the metal tapers evenly from the center of the design out to the edges and the point. If the edges of the design on the end of the metal are a little uneven, true them up with a file. Hammer the edges again with very light blows to remove any indications of file marks. In addition to the surface texture obtained with a ball-peen hammer, other very interesting effects can be secured on the ends of the metal by using a cross-peen or straight-peen hammer.

DECORATING THE SURFACE OF METAL

Many interesting and decorative textures can be produced on the surface of metal by hammering it with a ball-peen, cross-peen, or straight-peen hammer. The effect can also be varied by using different size hammers and controlling the force of the blow.

To decorate the surface, mark the area of the metal to be peened or hammered. Select the hammer that will produce the desired texture, Fig. 4-75.

BALL-PEEN   STRAIGHT-PEEN   CROSS-PEEN

Fig. 4-75. Suggested surface decorations for band iron.

Fig. 4-76. Peening the surface of metal.

Holding the metal with one hand, place it on the surface of a flat bench plate or anvil, Fig. 4-76. Strike the metal with firm, even blows, that touch one another. Do not pound the metal so hard that it stretches. Keep the blows firm and evenly spaced, working from one edge to the other. Continue this procedure, working from one end of the metal to the other filling in the space to be decorated. The metal will probably tend to bend out of shape as you peen. To straighten the metal, place it on a flat surface and strike it with a wood mallet.

If it is necessary to decorate the other side, place a piece of soft copper on the anvil. Lay the peened side

of the metal on the copper, and follow the procedure used in peening the first side. Slightly heavier blows will be necessary to obtain the same texture as that produced on the first side.

SMOOTHING METAL SURFACES WITH ABRASIVES

Metal projects are more attractive when properly finished. An appropriate finish adds to the quality of craftsmanship. To obtain a beautiful, finely polished piece of work is not difficult if a few general rules are kept in mind.

Most metals will take a fine polish if the proper abrasive is used. An abrasive is a material that cuts away other materials that are softer than itself. Abrasives may be selected from coarse grits that are fast cutting, to powders as fine as talcum that can be used for polishing.

There are two types of abrasives. Natural abrasives which are found in a natural state and artificial abrasives which are man-made. Emery and corundum are commonly used natural abrasives. Emery is about 60 percent aluminum oxide and 40 percent iron oxide. Corundum is about 85 percent aluminum oxide and 15 percent iron oxide.

Artificial abrasives are more commonly used on metal. There are two principal artificial abrasives, Silicon Carbide and Aluminum Oxide. Silicon carbide is made by heating coke, sawdust, salt, and pure silica sand to a high temperature, in an electric furnace. Aluminum oxide is made from bauxite ore, similar to that used in refining aluminum. It is also made in an electric furnace.

Abrasive materials which come from the furnace are in chunk form. These chunks are crushed into small particles--grits or grains. The size of an abrasive grain is determined by the size screen they will pass through. For example, if the screen has 46 openings per inch, the grains that just pass through are size 46. Abrasive grains range in size from 4 to 280. Abrasive flours, which are powdery fine, range from 280 to 600.

SELECTING ABRASIVES

There are many types of abrasives which are produced for various kinds of work. The most common type used in the school shop is abrasive cloth. This can be purchased in sheets 9 x 11 in. or in rolls 1/2 inch to 3 in. wide. For most bench metal work the following grain sizes are recommended:

> No. 60 - medium coarse
> No. 80 - medium
> No. 120 - medium fine
> No. 180 - fine

After the work has been carefully filed, a good polish can be obtained by rubbing first with No. 60, and then with No. 80 or finer. For a very high polish, use No. 120, and polish with No. 180. Abrasive cloth is used when it is not necessary to remove a quantity of metal.

When using abrasive cloth to do hand polishing follow this procedure:

1. Tear a piece of abrasive cloth from a sheet or roll.
2. Wrap it around a wood block which is long enough to grip comfortably, Fig. 4-77.
3. Apply a few drops of oil to the surface being polished. Rub the abrasive cloth back and forth. Do not allow the piece of metal with abrasive cloth to rock. Keep it flat against the surface being polished. To polish concave surfaces, wrap abrasive cloth around a rod that is smaller than the curvature of the surface. When polishing convex surfaces, use a strip of abrasive cloth and your fingers, Fig. 4-78.

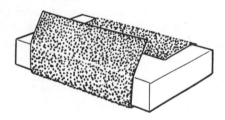

Fig. 4-77. Use abrasive cloth wrapped around a wood block to smooth flat surfaces.

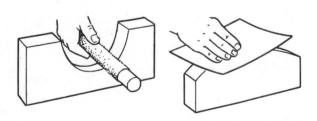

Fig. 7-78. Polishing concave and convex surfaces.

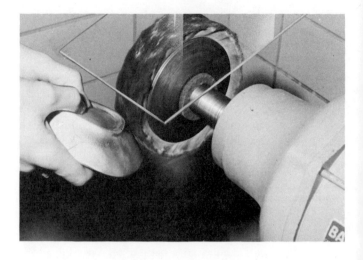

Fig. 4-79. Buffing metal.

BUFFING

Some projects in metalwork require a very highly polished surface. This can be done by using a buffing wheel and a buffing agent, Fig. 4-79. Buffing is not done until all visible tool marks and deep scratches have been removed with abrasive cloth as previously described. There are two basic types of buffing compounds: cutting compounds and burnishing compounds. Tripoli is one of the common cutting compounds that is used as a buffing agent. Tripoli is made from limestone having a high silica content. The silica grains are very soft and porous. For shop use, the powder is mixed with a grease base to form a stick or cake. Red and white rouge are two common burnishing (or coloring) compounds.

SAMMY SAFETY
SAYS:

"Before using the buffer, remove jewelry from your fingers and wrist. Roll your sleeves above your elbows. Place a face shield or safety glasses over your eyes."

The following procedure is used for buffing metal:

1. Turn the buffer motor on and apply a stick of polishing compound lightly against the face of wheel. Hold the compound below the center of

the wheel so it will tend to pull the compound toward the machine. After the wheel has been loaded with buffing compound add more compound sparingly as needed. Too much compound on the wheel will cause it to stick and build up on the metal being buffed. A different buffing wheel should be used when changing grades of compound. Mark the buffing wheels for the grades of compounds being used so they will not get mixed.

2. Grip the work securely with both hands and press it firmly against the rotating wheel. Be sure to keep the work below the center of the wheel. Move the work back and forth across the face of wheel as you buff the surface.

3. After the polishing has been completed, wash the work with soap and hot water. Dry with a soft clean cloth. Be careful not to touch the metal with your hands.

4. To maintain a high luster, coat the work immediately with clear lacquer, plastic, or wax.

CUTTING THREADS

The cutting of threads on metal rods (called external threads) and on the interior of holes drilled in metal (called interior threads) is an important phase of metalwork. The metalworker uses threads to transmit motion, to provide for adjustments, and to fasten parts together.

The American National thread system is the most common one used in the United States. The American National is a 60 degree thread with the crest and root flattened. Fig. 4-80. There are two common series. The National Course (NC), which is used for general purpose work, and the National Fine (NF) which is used for precision assemblies such as aircraft engines, automobiles, and adjusting mechanisms.

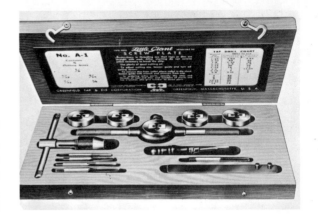

Fig. 4-81. A set of taps and dies.
(Greenfield Tap and Die Corp.)

Taps and dies are the tools used for cutting threads. Taps are used for cutting threads on the interior of holes. Dies are used to cut threads on the surface of metal rods. Fig. 4-81 shows a set of taps and dies.

CUTTING INTERNAL THREADS

A tap is a piece of hardened steel which has a threaded portion for cutting threads. The shank of the tap has a square end which is gripped by the tap wrench that is used to turn the tool. Hand taps are usually provided in sets of three taps for each diameter and thread series. Each set contains a taper tap, a plug tap, and a bottoming tap, Fig. 4-82. The taper tap is used to start or cut threads completely through open holes, Fig. 48-83a. To thread a partly open hole, start with a taper tap and finish the

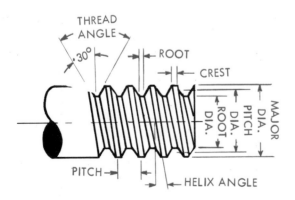

Fig. 4-80. Parts of a thread.

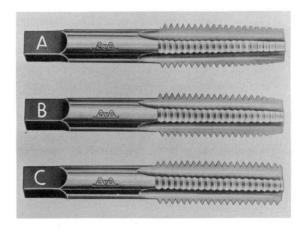

Fig. 4-82. Set of taps. (A) Taper; (B) Plug; (C) Bottoming.

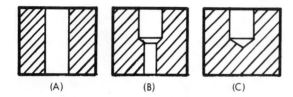

Fig. 4-83. Kinds of holes to be threaded. (A) Open hole; (B) Partly open hole; (C) Closed hole.

Size of Tap		Size of Tap Drill				Clearance Drill	
National Coarse	National Fine	Number Drills	Letter Drills	Fractional Drills	Decimal Equivalent	Drill Size	Decimal Equivalent
#4-40		43			0.0890	#31	0.1200
	#4-48	42			0.0935	#31	0.1200
#5-40		38			0.1015	#29	0.1360
	#5-44	37			0.1040	#29	0.1360
#6-32		36			0.1065	#25	0.1495
	#6-40	33			0.1130	#25	0.1495
#8-32		29			0.1360	#16	0.1770
	#8-36	29			0.1360	#16	0.1770
#10-24		25			0.1495	13/64	0.2031
	#10-32	21			0.1590	13/64	0.2031
#12-24		16			0.1770	7/32	0.2187
	#12-28	14			0.1820	7/32	0.2187
1/4"-20		7			0.2010	17/64	0.2656
	1/4"-28	3			0.2130	17/64	0.2656
5/16"-18		...	F		0.2570	21/64	0.3281
	5/16"-24	...	I		0.2720	21/64	0.3281
3/8"-16		...		5/16	0.3125	25/64	0.3906
	3/8"-24	...	Q		0.3320	25/64	0.3906
7/16"-14		...	U		0.3680	29/64	0.4531
	7/16"-20	...		25/64	0.3906	29/64	0.4531
1/2"-13		...		27/64	0.4219	33/64	0.5156
	1/2"-20	...		29/64	0.4531	33/64	0.5156
9/16"-12		...		31/64	0.4844	37/64	0.5781
	9/16"-18	...		33/64	0.5156	37/64	0.5781
5/8"-11		...		17/32	0.5312	41/64	0.6406
	5/8"-18	...		37/64	0.5781	41/64	0.6406
3/4"-10		...		21/32	0.6562	49/64	0.7656
	3/4"-16	...		11/16	0.6875	49/64	0.7656
7/8"-9		...		49/64	0.7656	57/64	0.8906
	7/8"-14	...		13/16	0.8125	57/64	0.8906
1"-8		...		7/8	0.8750	1 1/64	1.0156
	1"-14	...		15/16	0.9375	1 1/64	1.0156

Fig. 4-85. Tap drill sizes.

threading with a plug tap, Fig. 4-83b. To cut threads to the bottom of a closed hole, start the threading with the taper tap, then use the plug tap, and finish the threading operation with the bottoming tap, Fig. 4-83c. The tap size is stamped on the shank. For example, in the N.C. and N.F. series, if the tap is stamped 1/4 - 20 N.C., it means that the thread is 1/4 in. in diameter, there are 20 threads per inch and it is National Course. Taps are held in tap wrenches while they are being used. There are two types--the T-handle that is used for small taps, and the adjustable tap wrench that is used for larger sizes, Fig. 4-84.

Fig. 4-84. Tap wrenches. Above. T-handle tap wrench. Below. Adjustable tap wrench.

Following is the procedure for tapping a hole:

1. Select the correct size tap with the desired number of threads per inch.
2. Select the correct size tap drill. Refer to Fig. 4-85. If the exact letter or number drill is not available, use the next larger fractional drill shown in Fig. 4-43.
3. Drill the hole carefully.
4. Secure the tap in the tap wrench. Insert the tap in the hole and start turning the tap in a clockwise direction, Fig. 4-86. Apply enough downward

Fig. 4-86. Cutting internal threads.

pressure to start the tap cutting.
5. Check the tap to see if it is starting square with the hole. Remove tap wrench and check work with a square, Fig. 4-87. If the alignment of the tap is out of square, correct the error by applying sidewise pressure as you continue turning the tap.

Fig. 4-87. Checking a tap after it is started to make sure it is square with the piece.

Fig. 4-88. Left. Die. Right. Die stock.
(Greenfield Tap and Die Corp.)

6. If the hole is being tapped in steel apply a lubricant. Lard oil can be used. Cast iron is tapped dry.
7. Turn the tap forward about one-half turn, then back it up until you feel the chips break loose. Repeat this procedure until threading has been completed. When tapping cast iron the tap should not be backed but you should continue forward until threading is completed. CAUTION: Be careful not to force tap if it gets stuck. Taps are very brittle and will break easily. Gently move the tap back and forth until it loosens.
8. Remove the tap by backing it out carefully. If it gets stuck, work it back and forth gently to loosen.

When cutting threads in a partly open or closed hole, be very careful as the tap comes close to the bottom of the hole. Remove the tap and clean out the chips often, so the tap can reach the bottom of the hole.

Fig. 4-89. Left. Adjustable die. Right. Solid die.

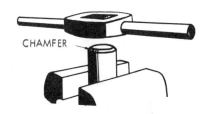

Fig. 4-90. Die will start more easily if the end is chamfered.

CUTTING EXTERNAL THREADS

External threads are cut by hand with a die held in a die stock, Fig. 4-88. The die cuts threads on the external surface of rods and bolts that will fit into standard-size nuts, tapped holes, or fittings. Some dies are adjustable while others are solid dies which are not adjustable, Fig. 4-89. Following is the procedure for cutting external threads:

1. Chamfer the end of the stock, Fig. 4-90. The chamfer can be cut with a file or on a grinder.
2. Select the correct size die for the diameter of the rod to be threaded. An N.C. or N.F. die can be used. When the number of threads per inch is not

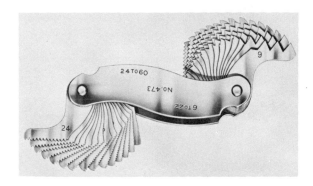

Fig. 4-91. A screw pitch gauge.
(L. S. Starrett Co.)

known, use a screw pitch gauge, Fig. 4-91. This gauge contains several thin blades which have saw like teeth on them. To use the gauge, try blades until one is found that fits the threads to be duplicated. The number of threads per inch is stamped on the blades.

3. Place the die in the die stock. Tighten the setscrews in the die stock, so the die is held firmly in place. If the die is adjustable, set it to cut oversize threads first. You can always make the threads smaller but you cannot make them larger. A tap is not adjustable, so it is better to tap first, then cut the external threads to fit the tapped hole.

4. Fasten the work firmly in a vise in a vertical or horizontal position.

5. Place the die over the end of work. Die threads are tapered. Be sure the tapered side starts the cut. Reverse the die only when it is necessary to cut full threads up to a square shoulder.

6. Start cutting the threads by turning the die stock clockwise and applying downward pressure. Be careful to start the threads straight and keep them straight. Add a little cutting oil when threading steel. Back up the die occasionally to break the chips loose. Continue until threading is completed.

7. Check the threaded work to see if it fits the tapped hole or nut. If the threads are too tight, adjust the die to take a little deeper cut and run the die over the threaded section again.

METAL FASTENING DEVICES

Fastening devices are used to hold pieces of a project together. The type, shape, and size of fastening devices to be used depend upon the nature of the work. For example, rivets are used to hold pieces together permanently. Bolts or screws are used when the pieces may be disassembled occasionally or have to be adjusted.

RIVETING

Rivets can be used for ornamentation as well as fastening pieces of metal together. Soft iron rivets are

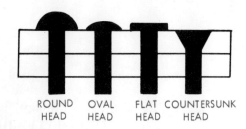

Fig. 4-92. Common rivet shapes.

used for wrought iron projects. They are available in round, oval, flat, and countersunk heads, Fig. 4-92. The most common size rivets used are 1/8 and 3/16 in. in diameter and 1 in. long. Projects made of aluminum, copper, or brass may be fastened together with rivets made of the same material, or contrasting metal. The most common size nonferrous rivets are 1/16 and 1/8 in. in diameter with round heads. The procedure for riveting is as follows:

1. Select the correct size and shape rivets. Use a flat-head rivet if it is not to be noticeable. Round-head rivets are used if they are to be part of the design. The rivets must be long enough to go through both pieces of metal and extend beyond by one and one-half times the diameter if the head is to be rounded on both sides. If the rivet is to be flush, allow just enough material to stick through to fill the countersunk hole.

2. Locate and drill the holes. Countersink the hole if the rivet is to be flush with the surface. If several rivets are to be used, drill only one hole and finish the riveting process before drilling the other holes. This procedure makes it easier to line up the remaining holes when joining two pieces.

3. Insert the rivet in the hole, and place the head against a solid piece of material. The heads of countersunk rivets should be set on an anvil or block of iron, and round-head rivets should rest in a cup-shaped hole so the shape of the head will not be damaged, Fig. 4-93. To rivet scroll work, place

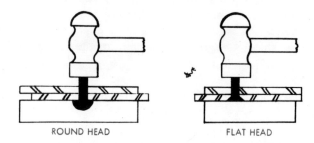

ROUND HEAD   FLAT HEAD

Fig. 4-93. Use a riveting plate or riveting set to protect the heat of the rivet.

the piece to be riveted over a steel rod fastened in a vise or to a bench, Fig. 4-94.

4. Upset the rivet by striking the end with the flat face of the ball-peen hammer, Fig. 4-95. This causes the rivet to expand and fill up the holes. If the rivet is to be formed, shape the flattened end of rivet by striking it with the peen end of the hammer. If the back of the rivet is to be flat, strike

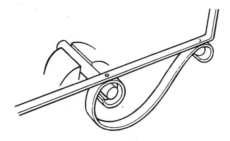

Fig. 4-94. A rod fastened in a vise can be used to rivet scroll work.

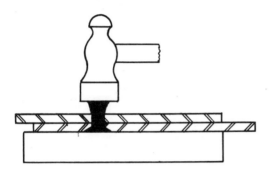

Fig. 4-95. Upsetting a rivet.

it with the peen end of the hammer to fill countersunk hole. Then finish operation by striking with the flat face of the hammer.

MACHINE SCREWS

Machine screws are used in tapped holes for the assembly of metal parts. Sometimes machine screws are used with nuts. Most machine screws are made of steel or brass. They can be purchased in a variety of diameters, lengths, and head shapes. Here is a typical example of how to give the specifications for a machine screw: 1 inch (length), 6-32 (thread-diameter), round head (head shape), steel (material). 6-32 means that the screw gauge is No. 6, and that it has 32 threads per inch. Most of the time you will use the common types of machine screws shown in Fig. 4-96.

ROUND HEAD   FILLISTER   FLAT HEAD
              HEAD

Fig. 4-96. Common types of machine screws.

Square or hex nuts can be used on machine screws. The head of a machine screw may be specified either slotted, for use with a plain screwdriver, or with a Phillips head for use with a special Phillips screwdriver.

STOVE BOLTS

Stove bolts were developed for use on stoves as the name suggests. They are used for many other jobs where accuracy and strength are not required. Stove bolts have coarse threads that make a loose fit with the threads of the square nut. Stove bolts can be purchased with flat heads, round heads, or oval heads.

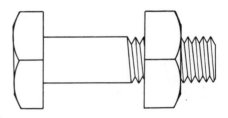

Fig. 4-97. Machine bolt.

MACHINE BOLTS

Machine bolts are made with square or hexagonal heads, and the nuts may also be of either type, Fig. 4-97. They may be purchased in a variety of diameters, lengths, and standard N.C. or N.F. threads. They can be furnished in three grades--rough, semi-finished, or machine-finished.

NUTS

Square and hexagonal nuts are standard, but there are also many special nuts available, Fig. 4-98. One of

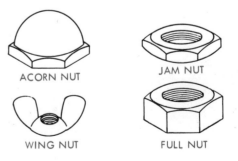

ACORN NUT   JAM NUT

WING NUT   FULL NUT

Fig. 4-98. Nuts.

these is the wing nut which is used where frequent adjustment is necessary. Cap, or acorn nuts are used when appearance is important. A jam nut is used on top of a standard hexagonal nut to lock it in position.

Fig. 4-99. Two common types of washers.

WASHERS

There are two common types of washers, the flat and the split lock, Fig. 4-99. Flat washers serve the function of providing larger bearing surfaces and preventing damage to the surfaces of the metal parts through which a bolt passes. Split lock washers are used under nuts to prevent them from loosening by vibration.

QUIZ — UNIT 4

1. Why is bench metal basic to all other areas of metalwork?
2. List four things a combination square can be used for in metalwork.
3. How can the surface of a piece of metal be prepared so scribed lines may be seen more clearly?
4. How many hacksaw teeth should be in contact with the metal when cutting?
5. What is a cold chisel used for?
6. Which method of filing should be used to obtain a smooth surface?
7. Name three systems used to designate the size of drills.
8. When drilling holes larger than 3/8 in. it is good practice to drill a _____ first.
9. If you are using 1/8 in. thick band iron and you are going to make two right angle bends, how much should be added to the length of the stock?
10. If a piece of pipe requires a sharp bend it should be filled with _____ or _____.
11. What is the difference between natural and artificial abrasives?
12. Which abrasive is the finest, No. 80 or No. 120?
13. Tripoli is a cutting compound that is used as a _____.
14. The American National thread is a _____ degree thread.
15. Internal threads can be cut by hand with a hand _____.
16. What is the difference between the tap drill size and the clearance drill size?
17. External threads can be cut by hand with a _____.
18. List four metal-fastening devices.

Industry provides many careers from the semi-skilled to the highly skilled sheet metal trades. The machine on the right side of the picture is a 600 ton stamping press. This company manufactures heating and air conditioner components. (Lennox Industries)

SHEET METAL

1. **The sheet metal industry.**
2. **How to use sheet metal tools and machines.**
3. **How to fabricate sheet metal projects.**

THE FIELD OF SHEET METAL WORK

This area of metalworking is concerned mostly with the building trades. It includes the installation of heating and air conditioning systems, roof work, and metal trim. Sheet metal work is also required in manufacturing automobiles, rockets, railroad cars, ships, airplanes, metal furniture, and household appliances.

In this area of metalwork you will learn to cut, form, shape, and assemble sheet metal stock. You will learn to make such items as boxes, pans, funnels, mailboxes, and canister sets. Most craftsmen find sheet metal work very interesting. It is also a fascinating hobby. Some of the fundamentals you studied in Unit 4, will be used in this unit.

CAREER OPPORTUNITIES

The sheet metal field and its related areas of work employ several million metalworkers. People employed in the sheet metal trades work mostly with sheet metal stock (black and galvanized), tin plate, copper, brass, and aluminum. They use sheets of metal ranging from a few thousandths to one inch or more in thickness. The sheet metal industry and the craftsmen who work in it contribute much to make life more comfortable and enjoyable.

The sheet metal worker lays out and plans the job. He determines the size and type of metal to be used and methods of fabrication. Sheet metal workers must be able to use hand snips, power driven shears, and other types of cutting tools with accuracy. He shapes the metal with a variety of hammers, anvils, and machines. The skilled craftsman in this field of work must also know how to weld, bolt, rivet, solder, or cement seams and joints. Some journeymen specialize in shopwork or on-site installation work. However, the skilled sheet metal worker must be able to perform all of the operations required.

LAYING OUT AND DEVELOPING PATTERNS

Before constructing a sheet metal project it is necessary to first develop a stretchout (pattern) either on a sheet of paper, or on the metal. The inexperienced sheet metal worker should draw the pattern on paper first so it can be checked to see if any mistakes have been made. The pattern is then transferred to the metal by scribing the lines directly on the metal. Use a pencil if a scriber mark is objectionable. If several pieces of the same kind are to be made and especially where irregular curves are involved, a metal template is used. This template is placed on the metal and a scriber is used to trace around the outside.

Many sheet metal articles require developments. The three kinds of pattern development include: Parallel-line development, as shown in Fig. 5-1,

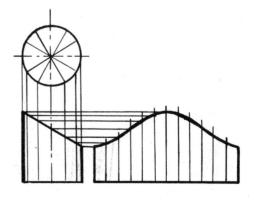

Fig. 5-1. Parallel-line development. This kind of pattern development may be used to lay out a scoop.

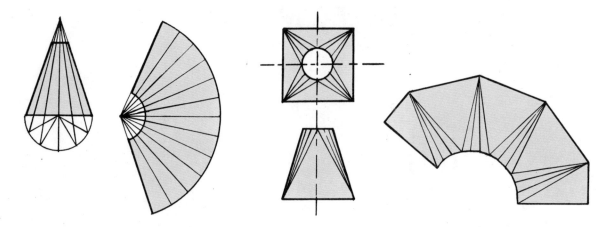

Fig. 5-2. Left. Radial-line development that might be used for a funnel. Fig. 5-3. Right. A combination of parallel-line and radial-line development. This kind of pattern development is used when it is necessary to go from square to round, as in heating and ventilating duct work.

Radial-line development, Fig. 5-2, and a combination of Parallel-line and Radial-line development, Fig. 5-3. The latter of these includes triangles as well as cones and cylinders, and is sometimes referred to as triangulation. Refer to Unit 11, in the Build-A-Course Series on Drafting which explains how to develop sheet metal patterns.

CUTTING SHEET METAL

Sheet metal which is 18-ga. or less in thickness, can be cut with bench shears. The standard tinner's snips will cut metal 22-ga. or lighter. Some of the more common snips are: Straight snips which are for cutting straight lines and to cut on the outside of large curves, Fig. 5-4; Hawk-billed snips which have

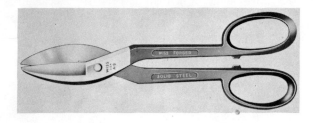

Fig. 5-4. Straight snips.   (J. Wiss & Sons Co.)

narrow, curved blades and are used for making curved cuts; Aviation snips which are very useful for making various types of cuts, Fig. 5-5. Aviation snips are very handy for cutting compound curves and intricate designs. They are made in three styles--the right,

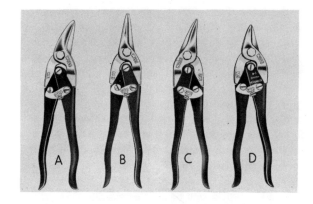

Fig. 5-5. Aviation snips. (A) cuts to the left; (B) cuts to the right; (C) cuts straight or curved; (D) is used for notching.

which cuts to the right; the left, which cuts to the left; and the universal, which cuts either right or left.

When cutting with snips, never cut with the full length of the blades. If the blades of the snips are completely closed, the points will tear the metal sidewise where they meet. Stop each cut approximately 1/4 in. from the end of the blades, and start the new cut with the throat. The throat is that part of the blades nearest to the pivot pin. Always cut to the right of the layout line when possible. When cutting outside curves, first rough out to within about 1/8 in. of the layout line with aviation snips. Then finish the work by carefully cutting around layout line, Fig. 5-6. To cut inside curves, first punch or drill a hole in the waste stock large enough to allow the blades of the hawk-bill snips to get started. Insert the snips from the underside of stock and rough cut the inside

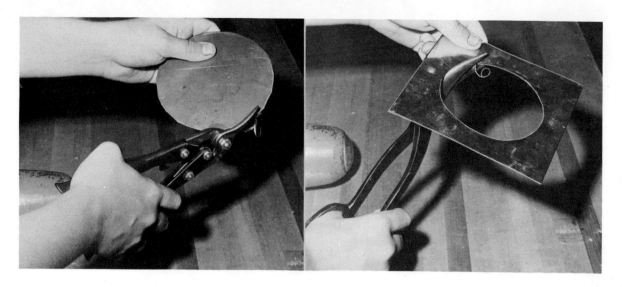

Fig. 5-6. Left. Cutting on outside curve with aviation snips. Fig. 5-7. Right, Cutting on inside opening with hawk-bill snips.

opening to within about 1/4 in. of the layout line. Then trim the hole to size, Fig. 5-7.

When the snip blades become dull, they can be sharpened by grinding. Take the two blades apart and grind them to an included angle of 85 deg. Put the blades together again and adjust the blade tension by turning the nut on the pivot bolt or pin. The blades should be just tight enough to remain in any position in which you open them. Keep the pivot well oiled. Keep the blades closed when the snips are not being used. Remember snips are sheet metal tools and should not be used to cut wires, bolts, rivets, or nails.

Fig. 5-8. Electric portable shears.

Electric portable shears are very handy for cutting sheet metal which is 18 ga. or lighter, Fig. 5-8. This machine can be used to make both straight and curved cuts. It will cut a minimum radius of about 1 in. To use the shears, place the metal between the cutters. Turn on the switch and guide the cutters along the line to be cut.

Some shops are equipped with squaring shears, Fig. 5-9. This machine can be used to trim and square sheet metal 18 ga. or lighter. The size of the machine is determined by the width of material it will cut. The common sizes are 30 or 36 in. To use the machine set the back gage at the rear of the shears to cut material to the desired length. Insert the material from the front and hold it firmly against the side and rear gages. Press the treadle down with your foot to make the cut. When the work is inserted from the back use the front gage to control the length of cut. The side gage which is adjustable should be kept at right angles to the cutting blade.

BENDING SHEET METAL

Sheet metal can be bent by hand or with a machine. A craftsman should know how to bend sheet metal by hand because machinery is not always available. Also, there are occasions where a machine in the shop does not have the necessary capacity to perform the operation.

BENDING BY HAND

To make angular bends by hand, clamp two pieces of hardwood or angle iron in a vise, with the sheet metal between them. If the metal is too large to fit in

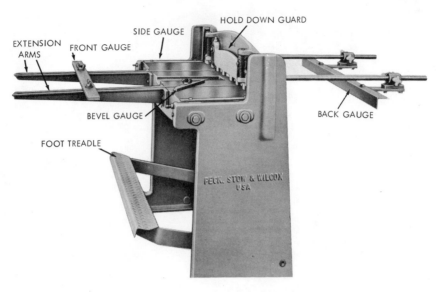

EXTENSION ARMS
FRONT GAUGE
SIDE GAUGE
HOLD DOWN GUARD
BACK GAUGE
BEVEL GAUGE
FOOT TREADLE

PECK, STOW & WILCOX
USA

Fig. 5-9. Squaring shears. (Peck, Stow & Wilcox Co.)

Fig. 5-10. Above. Metal clamped to bench for bending. Below. Bend the metal gradually working back and forth across the metal.

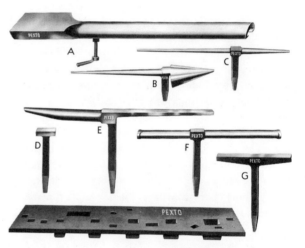

Fig. 5-11. Sheet metal stakes: (A) hollow mandrel; (B) blowhorn; (C) candle mould; (D) common square; (E) breakhorn; (F) double seaming; (G) hatchet; (H) stake plate. (Peck, Stow & Wilcox Co.)

the vise, use two C clamps, Fig. 5-10. The line where the metal is to be bent should be even with the upper edge of the jig. To bend the metal down, start by striking light blows with a mallet at one end and work along the full length of the stock. Continue working back and forth making a gradual bend.

There are several sheet metal stakes which can be used for many bending and forming operations, Fig. 5-11. A hatchet stake can be used to make a sharp angle bend. To bend metal this way, place the bend line of the piece over the sharp edge of the stake. Then press the metal down with your hands, Fig. 5-12a. Square up bend with a wood mallet, Fig. 5-12b.

To bend a box by hand, first clamp the metal as shown in Fig. 5-13a. Bend the hem at a right angle. Release the clamps and remove the metal. Clamp the

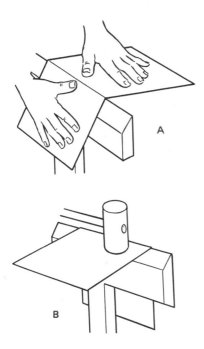

Fig. 5-14. Closing a hem with a mallet and block of wood.

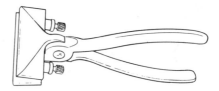

Fig. 5-15. A hand seamer.

Fig. 5-12. Making a sharp bend over a hatchet stake.

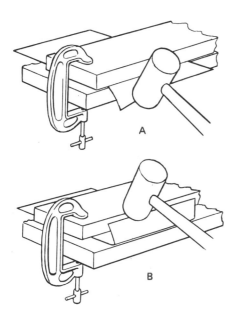

Fig. 5-13. Bending a hem between two boards.

piece against the top surface of a bench with one hand and grip the metal with the hand seamer. Squeeze the handles of the hand seamer so the jaws will not slip off the metal. Bend the hem as far as the seamer will allow it to go. Open the seamer and squeeze the metal to close the hem.

After the hems have been bent by one of the described methods, bend the two ends of the box by using clamps and two pieces of wood. Next, cut a block of wood the exact size of the bottom of the box. Clamp this block in position as shown in Fig. 5-16. Then bend up the sides of the box. Draw the metal tightly against the wood block by striking it with light blows near the bend with a mallet. Work back and forth across the full length of the bend. Be careful not to dent the metal with the edge of the mallet head.

SAMMY SAFETY
SAYS:

metal on the edge of a bench with the partially turned hem up, Fig. 5-13b. Close the hem with a mallet and a block of wood Fig. 5-14. A short hem can be made with a hand seamer, Fig. 5-15. First, adjust the hand seamer for the size hem to be bent by setting the knurled screws at the proper distance and clamp them in place with the locking nut. Press the

"When using Squaring Shears, keep your fingers away from the cutting blade at all times. When it is necessary to have a helper, warn him of the danger of getting his foot under the treadle or his hands near the cutting blade."

Fig. 5-16. Bending up the sides of a box by hand. Above. Metal clamped in position for bending. Below. Drawing the metal tightly against the block of wood with a mallet.

BENDING CYLINDRICAL FORMS BY HAND

A cylindrical piece may be formed to shape by bending it around a stake, rod, or pipe which is

Fig. 5-17. Forming light weight metal around a rod by hand.

slightly smaller or equal to the diameter to be bent. Light-weight metal can be formed around the stake by hand, Fig. 5-17. To form heavier weights, hold the metal on top of a stake with one hand, then strike it glancing blows with a mallet as you feed the piece across the stake, Fig. 5-18. Continue this procedure until the metal has been formed to the desired shape.

Fig. 5-18. Forming heavier weight metal around a rod with a mallet.

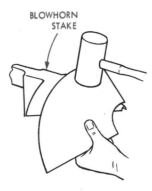

Fig. 5-19. Forming metal over a blowhorn stake.

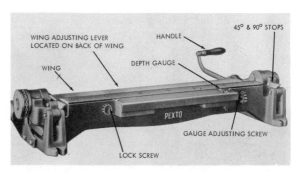

Fig. 5-20. A bar folder.   (Peck, Stow & Wilcox Co.)

FORMING CONE-SHAPED ARTICLES

Cone-shaped pieces such as funnels and spouts should be formed on a tapered stake. A funnel, for example, can be formed over the apron of a blowhorn stake, Fig. 5-19. When the gage of the metal is too heavy to form by hand use a mallet.

BENDING METAL ON A BAR FOLDER

The bar folder is a folding machine which comes in various sizes, the most common of which has a folding length of 30 in. Fig. 5-20. These machines will fold an edge as narrow as 1/8 to 1 in. on metal as heavy as 24 gage. A 3/16 in. fold is the narrowest bend practicable when using 22 ga. metal.

The bar folder is used for making single or double hems, a sharp or open lock, turning an edge to receive a wire, and turning flanges, Fig. 5-21. To perform

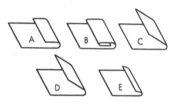

Fig. 5-21. Common hems that can be turned on the bar folder: (A) single hem; (B) double hem; (C) sharp lock; (D) open lock; (E) turned edge to receive a wire.

these operations there are two adjustments to make. The depth of the fold which is controlled by turning the gage-adjusting screw knob in or out, and the sharpness of the fold which is obtained by adjusting the wing. There are two angle stops at the left end of the bar folder. By setting the appropriate angle stop in place the fold may be stopped at 45 or 90 deg. The fold can be stopped at any desired angle from 10 to 120 deg. by setting the adjustable stop at the handle end of the machine.

In preparing to use the bar folder, check the edge of the metal to be folded to be sure it is straight, then follow this procedure:

1. Loosen the locking screw, then turn the gage-adjusting screw until the machine is set to make a fold of the desired width. Tighten the locking screw to hold this adjustment.
2. Loosen the wedge screw on the folding bar and position the wing with the wing-adjusting lever to make an open or closed lock as desired. Tighten the wedge screw to hold this adjustment. When making an open lock for wired edges, set the wing adjusting lever so the distance between the wing and the edge of the folding blade is equal to the diameter of the wire plus about 1/32 in. Set the gage to make a fold equal to one and one-half times the wire diameter.
3. Place the edge of the metal in the folder and hold it against the gage tightly. Then pull the handle toward you until the fold is completed, Fig. 5-22. Do not release your grip on the handle until it is in its original position.
4. Return the handle to starting position. Remove the folded metal.
5. If a hem is being made, place the metal on the beveled part of the blade with the fold upward, and set tightly against the wing of the folder, Fig. 5-23. Pull the handle to flatten the fold. Return the handle to its original position, and remove the metal.

BENDING METAL ON A BOX AND PAN BRAKE

The Box and Pan Brake is an ideal machine for bending metal boxes and pans of a size within its limits, Fig. 5-24. Most box and pan brakes found in school shops will bend metal up to 24 in. long, and 16 ga. in thickness. The upper jaw is made up of removable fingers which are of various widths. To bend a box on this machine, fold the hems first. Then fold the two sides at 90 deg. To bend the two ends,

Fig. 5-22. Left. Folding metal in the bar folder. Fig. 5-23. Right. Closing a hem on the bar folder.

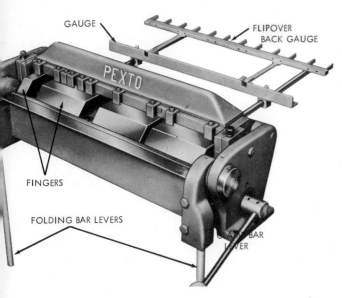

GAUGE
FLIPOVER
BACK GAUGE
PEXTO
FINGERS
FOLDING BAR LEVERS

Fig. 5-24. A box and pan brake.

set up the machine with just enough fingers to equal the width of the box. Bend the two ends. Many shapes can be bent on a Box and Pan Brake.

FORMING METAL ON A FORMING MACHINE

The forming machine, or rolls, as they are more commonly called, are used for curving sheet metal and forming cylinders of various diameters. The most common forming machines have rolls that are 30 to 36 in. wide and 2 in. in diameter, Fig. 5-25. They can

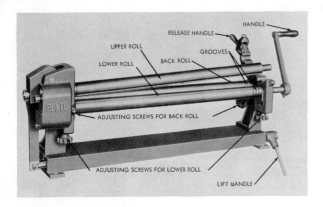

HANDLE
RELEASE HANDLE
UPPER ROLL
GROOVES
LOWER ROLL
BACK ROLL
PEXTO
ADJUSTING SCREWS FOR BACK ROLL
ADJUSTING SCREWS FOR LOWER ROLL
LIFT HANDLE

Fig. 5-25. Forming rolls. (Peck, Stow & Wilcox Co.)

form mild steel sheet metal as heavy as 22 ga. This machine has three rolls. The two front rolls grip the sheet of metal and force it against the rear roll, which bends it upward curving the sheet and forming the cylinder. The lower front roll can be adjusted for

different thicknesses of metal. The back roll can be raised or lowered to form different diameter cylinders. The back roll can also be set at an angular, vertical position for forming tapered cylinders. To form a cylinder follow this procedure:

1. Adjust the lower front roller up or down so there is just enough clearance between the two front rolls for the sheet metal to slip in under slight pressure.
2. The back roll is then adjusted to a position which will form the cylinder. There is no set rule that may be applied for setting the rear roll. Some metals have more spring than others. Therefore, the adjustment of the rear roll can best be obtained by experimenting. The back roll must be parallel to the front rolls.
3. Insert the sheet metal from the front of the machine between the two front gripping rolls. Turn the hand crank and feed the metal through the front rolls and against upper side of the rear forming roll which bends the metal upward forming the cylinder, Fig. 5-26.

Fig. 5-26. Back roll beginning to form a cylinder.

4. Continue turning the hand crank to shape the cylinder. Readjust the back roll if the cylinder is not the correct radius. Lowering the rear forming roll will increase the diameter of the cylinder, and raising the rear forming roll will decrease the diameter of the cylinder.
5. Remove formed cylinder from rolls, Fig. 5-27.

To form cone-shaped pieces on the forming machine, adjust the front rolls as before. Set the rear roll at an angle that is approximately the same as the taper of the cone, with the left end of the roll nearer the front rolls. Insert the metal with the long side to the right. Hold the short side of the metal so it will go

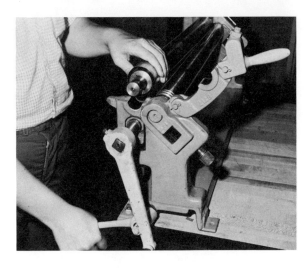

Fig. 5-27. Removing a cylinder from the forming rolls.

Fig. 5-28. Forming a piece of metal in the rolls with a wired edge.

through the rolls more slowly than the long side as the cone is formed.

The grooves of varying sizes in the right end of the lower and rear rolls are for forming cylinders which have a wired edge, Fig. 5-28. The procedure for forming wired edge metal is the same as described before, except when forming wired material heavier or lighter than 20 ga. When forming wired material heavier than 20 ga. the rear roll of the forming machine must be set at a distance that is slightly greater at the wired end than at the opposite end. Wired material lighter than 20 ga. requires an adjustment that provides a distance between the rear roll and both the upper and lower rolls that is greater at the wired end than at the opposite end.

SHEET METAL SEAMS

A great many methods are employed to strengthen and join pieces of sheet metal. Some of the common

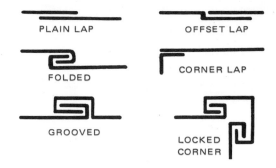

Fig. 5-29. Some of the common sheet metal seams.

seams are shown in Fig. 5-29. Lap seams are generally used in the construction of rectangular objects and small diameter cylinders. Lap seams are usually riveted or soldered. Folded seams are generally used when laying flat seam metal roofing. A folded seam is made by turning single edges on the two pieces of the sheet metal that are to be joined, Fig. 5-30. Allow

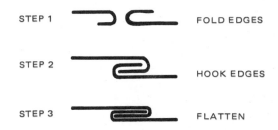

Fig. 5-30. Steps in making a folded seam.

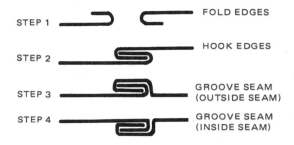

Fig. 5-31. Steps in making a grooved seam.

extra material equal to three times the seam width. Hook the two edges together and place the metal over a stake if the work is circular, or on a solid flat surface if the piece is flat. Hammer the seam flat with a wood mallet. Grooved seams are generally used in joining flat pieces of metal, making vertical side seams, in flaring or cylindrically shaped objects, and making longitudinal seams in square or round sheet metal pipes, Fig. 5-31. To make a grooved seam, follow the procedure given for making a folded seam up to the steps given for closing the seam. To close the seam, select a hand groover of the required size,

close the seam, Fig. 5-33. Continue working back and forth across the seam striking the groover moderate blows with a metal hammer to complete the seam. Fig. 5-34.

Fig. 5-32. A hand groover.

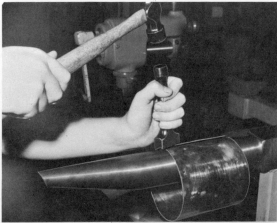

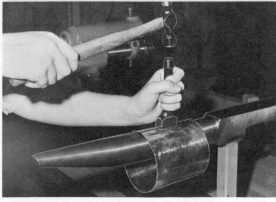

Fig. 5-33. Above. Locking the end of a seam. Fig. 5-34. Below. After both ends have been locked, complete the seaming operation by working back and forth across the seam, striking the groover moderate blows.

Fig. 5-32. Always use a hand groover approximately 1/16 in. wider than the finished seam. Place the piece on a suitable support. Set the groover exactly over one end of the seam. Strike the groover a firm blow to

Fig. 5-35. A combustion rotary machine with several sets of rolls.

USING A ROTARY MACHINE

A rotary machine consists mainly of a rigid cast iron frame fitted with shafts, gears, and several different sets of rolls, Fig. 5-35. This machine can be set up to perform beading, crimping, burring, wiring, and turning. To save time, some shops are equipped with a separate machine for each operation so the rolls do not have to be changed.

Wiring an edge on a rotary machine is accomplished by setting the machine up with various sets of rolls. Following is the procedure:

1. Determine the size of wire to be used.
2. Lay out stock, making allowance for the material needed to make the wired edge. The amount of extra stock needed for 22 ga. or lighter is equal to 2-1/2 times the diameter of the wire. For example, if the wire is 1/8 in. in diameter: 2-1/2 x 1/8 in. = 5/2 x 1/8 = 5/16 in.—the additional amount of stock required.
3. Cut stock to correct size. The edge to be wired must be perfectly straight.
4. Install the turning rolls on the rotary machine, Fig. 5-36.
5. Measuring from the center of the groove in the lower roller, set the gage a distance equal to two and one-half times the diameter of the wire.

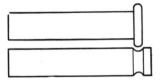

Fig. 5-36. A set of turning rolls.

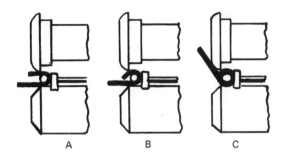

Fig. 5-38. Closing a wired edge.

6. Place the metal between the two rolls with the edge firmly against the gage, Fig. 5-37a.
7. Tighten the upper roll until it grips the metal. Turn the hand crank and feed the metal through the rolls until one complete turn has been made. Guide the metal carefully so the groove is even.
8. Lower the upper roll by tightening the crank screw about one-eighth of a turn. Tilt the work upward slightly as in Fig. 5-37b. Turn the crank until another complete revolution has been made.
9. Continue tightening the upper roll after each pass. Tilt the body of the work a little higher with each pass until a U-shaped groove is formed, Fig. 5-37c.

The next step is to install the wiring rolls, Fig. 5-38, on the machine and close the wired edge by following this procedure:

1. Select and cut a piece of wire of the correct diameter and length.
2. Adjust the gage a distance from the sharp edge of the upper roll equal to the diameter of the wire, plus twice the thickness of the metal.
3. Insert the wire in the seat formed with the turning rolls. Shape the wire so it will fit in the seat easily.
4. Place the article to be wired between the rolls, with the wired edge up, and against the gage, Fig. 5-38a. Lower the upper roll until the roll grips the work firmly.
5. Turn the crank until the edge being wired has traveled through the rolls.
6. Lower the upper roll a little farther and feed the

work through again. Continue this procedure until the metal is folded firmly around the wire. On the last pass, tilt the work upward slightly to force the edge of the metal under the wire.
7. Loosen the upper roll and remove the work.

Fig. 5-39. (A) Turning a flange; (B) Beading.

Burring rolls which are generally furnished with a rotary machine, are used to turn a flange on a cylinder, and to turn a burr on a bottom in making a double seam to attach to a cylinder, Fig. 5-39a. The beading rolls are used to decorate and strengthen the sides of sheet metal projects, Fig. 5-39b.

FASTENING SHEET METAL

There are several methods used to join sheet metal pieces together. You will want to become familiar with some of the most common processes by using them when you construct your projects. Procedure are given in this unit for riveting, soldering and the use of sheet metal screws.

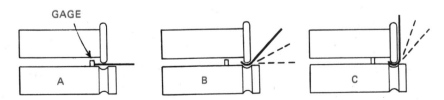

Fig. 5-37. Steps in using the turning rolls to form an edge to receive a wire.

RIVETING

Rivets are used to join two or more sheets of metal together permanently. The rivets used are generally made of aluminum, copper or iron. It is customary to use rivets of the same metal as the parts that are being joined. Round head and flat-head solid rivets are more commonly used. Tinner's rivets are used on thin black iron, galvanized iron, and tin plate. They have flat heads and are made of soft iron or steel. They are usually coated with tin as a protection against corrosion. The sizes are designated by the weight of 1,000 rivets. The length of a tinner's rivet is proportionate to its weight and diameter, Fig. 5-40. All rivets of one size are the same length.

| 10 OZ. | 12 OZ. | 1 LB. | 2 LB. | 3 LB. |

Fig. 5-40. Tinner's rivets (actual size).

The following procedure is generally used when riveting sheet metal:

1. Select the rivets to be used. The size rivet depends on the thickness (gage) of metal being joined and the diameter of the rivet shank. In general the rivet shank should extend from one to two diameters beyond the material. The diameter of the rivet should not be less than the total thickness of the pieces being joined.
2. Lay out the location for the rivets on the work-piece. All of the holes must be properly spaced and lined up. The spacing of rivets is determined by the type of material used and the nature of the work. For most practical purposes, a good rule is--minimum distance between rivets should be three diameters of the rivet shank, and the maximum, eight diameters. The distance from the edge of the work should be two diameters of the rivet shank.
3. Drill or punch the holes. Holes in thin metal are usually punched. Place metal over the end grain of a hardwood block or a lead block. Set the punch over the place where the hole is to be punched. Strike the punch solidly with a hammer to form the hole, Fig. 5-41. To be sure the holes in the pieces being joined will line up, drill or punch all of the holes in one of the pieces, and only one hole in the second piece. Join the two

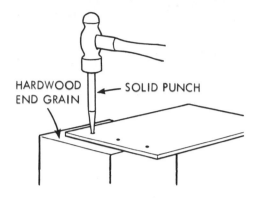

HARDWOOD END GRAIN — SOLID PUNCH

Fig. 5-41. Punching holes for rivets with a solid punch.

pieces with a rivet. Using the holes already drilled in the first piece as guides, drill the rest of the holes in the second piece.
4. Set the rivets. Place the rivet in the first hole with the head down on a flat, solid surface. If the work being riveted is cylindrical, place the rivet in the hole with the head of the rivet down on the crown of a stake. Place the hole of the rivet set over the rivet shank, Fig. 5-42a. Strike the

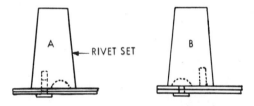

Fig. 5-42. (A) Setting a rivet; (B) Heading a rivet.

rivet set with a hammer to flatten the sheet metal around the hole and draw the sheets together. Keep the rivet set square with the surface of the sheet metal so it will not dent the work.
5. Head the rivet by striking the shank several direct blows with a hammer to expand the shank slightly beyond the hole. Form the head of the rivet by placing the cone-shaped depression of the rivet set in a vertical position over the shank. Then strike the rivet set with a hammer several times to round off the head, Fig. 5-42b. Be careful not to dent the sheet metal.

SHEET METAL SCREWS

Sheet metal screws are used in sheet metal work to join and install duct work for heating, ventilation, and air-conditioning. Many of our appliances are covered with sheet metal cases which are joined with sheet metal screws. These screws are known in the trade as self-tapping screws since they cut their own threads in mild and soft sheet metal. They are available in both sharp and blunt ends, Fig. 5-43. The

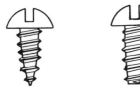

Fig. 5-43. Sheet metal screws. Left. Type A with sharp point. Right. Type Z with blunt point.

blunt-end screws are generally found to be most satisfactory, but the pointed type is used if alignment of holes is difficult. The sharp pointed screws are generally used to join material which is lighter than .050 in. thick. The blunt end screws are used for sheets from .015 to .203 in. thick. Sheet metal screws are available in several head shapes with either slotted or Phillips recessed heads.

Procedure for using sheet metal screws:

1. Lay out the holes and prick punch the locations.
2. Choose the correct size drill, Fig. 5-44 and Fig. 5-45. The drill size should equal the root diameter of the screw. Drill the hole.
3. Line up the hole and start the screw. Be sure the two pieces of metal are held together firmly. Then fasten the screw in place with a screwdriver.

SOFT SOLDERING

Soldering is the process of fastening two or more pieces of metal together by means of an alloy (solder) having a lower melting point than that of the pieces being joined. Soft solders are made of varying percentages of tin and lead. The most common compositions are 40/60, 50/50, and 60/40, (the first number mentioned is always tin). A good all-round solder contains 40 percent tin and 60 percent lead. This solder becomes completely liquid and mobile at 460 deg. F. Some craftsmen prefer 50/50 solder, also called "half and half." 50/50 solder becomes completely molten at 414 degrees F. Solder is available in bars, solid wire, and acid or rosin-core wire. The last two types have the flux in the center of the wire.

Screw Size	Metal Thickness	Drill Size No.
No. 4	.018	44
	.024	42
	.030	42
	.036	40
No. 6	.018	39
	.024	39
	.030	38
	.036	36
No. 8	.018	33
	.024	33
	.030	32
	.036	31
No. 10	.018	30
	.024	30
	.030	30
	.036	29

Fig. 5-44. Recommended drill sizes for self-tapping, sharp pointed sheet metal screws.

Screw Size	Metal Thickness	Drill Size No.
No. 4	.018	44
	.024	43
	.030	42
	.036	42
No. 6	.018	37
	.024	36
	.030	36
	.036	35
No. 8	.024	32
	.030	31
	.036	31
No. 10	.024	27
	.030	27
	.036	26

Fig. 5-45. Recommended drill sizes for self-tapping, blunt end sheet metal screws.

Fluxes are used to remove oxide from the metal, and to prevent the formation of new oxide. Flux also lowers the surface tension of the molten solder so it will flow easily and penetrate where it should. There are two classes of fluxes, corrosive and non-corrosive. The corrosive works best but must never be used on electrical connections. Corrosive flux must be washed from the metal with warm water after soldering. The non-corrosive flux is used for all electrical work. There are many commercially prepared liquid, powder, and paste fluxes available. These work very satisfactorily for school shop purposes when used as directed by the manufacturer.

Soldering requires a source of heat. A common method used to transmit heat to the metal surface being joined is by means of a soldering copper, Fig. 5-46. The working end of this tool is made of copper

Fig. 5-46. A soldering copper.

because it is an excellent conductor of heat. Soldering coppers are available in several weights. A copper weighing 1/2 lb. is best for light work, a 1 lb. copper for medium work, and a 1 1/2 lb. copper for heavier jobs. A gas bench furnace can be used to heat the soldering copper, Fig. 5-47. An electric copper with

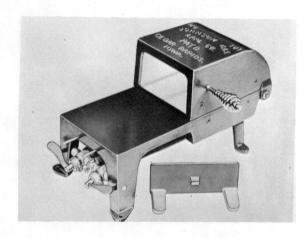

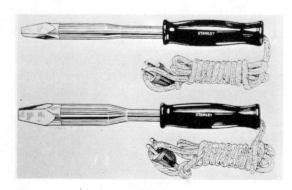

Fig. 5-48. Electric soldering iron.

interchangeable tips, Fig. 5-48, or a soldering gun, Fig. 5-49, is very convenient for light work and is especially good for soldering electrical connections.

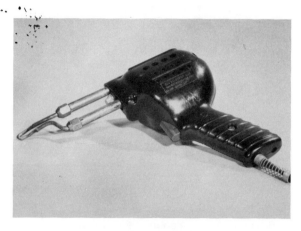

Fig. 5-49. A soldering gun.

Soldering coppers must be tinned before they will do a good job of soldering. After a soldering copper has been used for some time, or if it has been overheated the point becomes covered with oxide. This oxide prevents the heat from flowing to the metal. To tin a soldering copper follow this procedure:

1. File the faces of the point with a mill file until they are smooth, flat and clean.
2. Heat the copper until it is hot enough to melt the solder.
3. Rub the faces of the point on a sal-ammoniac block while the point is hot.
4. Apply a little solder to the point as it is rubbed on the sal-ammoniac. A thin, bright film called tin will form on the point if the copper is not over-heated.
5. Remove any excess molten solder from the point with a rag.

Liquid flux can be used instead of the sal-ammoniac for tinning by dipping the point into the flux and rubbing it with solder.

The following procedure should be followed to insure a strong, neat soldering job:

1. Clean the surfaces to be soldered. Solder will not stick to dirty, oily, or an oxide coated surface. Liquid cleaner can be used to clean a dirty

SAMMY SAFETY
SAYS:

"Avoid breathing fumes from the sal-ammoniac — they cause headaches and injure the lungs."

surface. Remove oxide from the metal with abrasive cloth.

2. Use a properly tinned copper.

3. Keep the surfaces to be joined close together to insure a strong bond, seam, or joint.

4. Flux only the area to be soldered. Be sure to use the proper flux for the job.

5. Heat the soldering copper to the proper temperature. Copper should be hot enough to melt solder readily. Do not allow it to become red-hot.

6. Tack the seam or joint by applying solder at several points. This is done by placing the point of the soldering copper on the metal where it is to be tacked. Hold it there until the flux sizzles. Then apply a small amount of solder to the metal directly in front of the point of the copper.

7. Place one face of the copper flat against the metal at one end. Hold it there until the solder melts, Fig. 5-50.

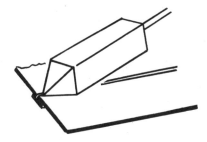

Fig. 5-50. Hold one face of the soldering copper flat against the surface of the metal.

8. Draw the copper SLOWLY along the seam or joint in one direction only, flowing the solder on in front of the point. The soldered joint or seam will not be satisfactory if the solder is just "stuck on" or melted on.

9. Do not move or handle the soldered job until the solder has "set" and has partially cooled. Solder is brittle and weak while solidifying.

10. If an acid flux has been used, wash off all traces of the flux with running warm water.

Sometimes it is necessary to solder several thicknesses of metal together or to apply one piece of metal to another so the solder will not show. This is called sweat soldering. In sweat soldering, the contacting surfaces of the metal is coated with a thin, even coating of solder. The surfaces are then placed together and heated with a large copper or a torch until the solder melts. This "sweats" the pieces of metal together. Use plenty of flux and be sure the pieces being joined are clean.

QUIZ — UNIT 5

1. List three major building trades that employ sheet metal workers.

2. In sheet metal work a development or pattern is called a _____ .

3. List three kinds of pattern development.

4. When cutting sheet metal that is 22 ga. or lighter you can use straight snips for _____ cuts and to cut large _____ curves.

5. Hawk-bill snips are used for making _____ cuts.

6. A hatchet stake can be used to make _____ bends.

7. A cone-shaped piece of metal can be formed over a _____ stake.

8. List four sheet metal operations that can be performed on a bar folder.

9. What is the function of the back roll of a forming machine?

10. What is a hand groover?

11. Figure the amount of material needed to make a wired edge on a piece of 22 ga. metal, using 1/16 in. wire.

12. The diameter of a sheet metal rivet should not be less than the _____ _____ of the pieces being joined.

13. A _____ _____ is used to "head" a rivet.

14. Sheet metal screws are available in both _____ and _____ ends.

15. What size drill should be used for a No. 6, sharp pointed sheet metal screw, to join metal that is .030 in. thick?

16. List four forms of solders.

17. Why must the oxide which forms on the point of a soldering copper be removed?

FORGING

1. **Forming metal by forging.**

2. **Forging tools and equipment.**

3. **Hand forging procedures.**

One of the earliest methods of forming iron was by hand forging. In hand forging, the metal is heated in a forge and shaped over an anvil with hammers and tools of various kinds. Today, industry has speeded up forging for production by using various kinds of machine-powered hammers or presses that are used instead of hand sledges. These machines can forge such items as tools, axles, and crankshafts for an automobile engine. Some of the jobs in a forge shop require skill in the operation of power hammers. People who operate power hammers are called hammersmiths. The hammer which moves up and down under power shapes the heated metal. The hammersmith controls both the strokes of the hammer and the movement of the metal as it is shaped.

You will find hand forging a very interesting area of metalwork. There is something facinating about hammering red-hot steel which is soft and plastic. You will also find forging useful in making repairs on metal parts around the home and in the shop.

CAREER OPPORTUNITIES

The basic equipment used in this field of work includes hand tools (hammers, tongs, and anvil with hardies), various types of power hammers, power forming and trimming presses, dies, and furnaces. A forging press or hammer generally is operated by a crew of two to ten men. The size of the crew depends on the work piece size and the operation to be performed.

Major forging occupations are as follows: Hammersmiths--interpret blueprints, determine the force of the hammer for the job, and decide the correct amount of heating needed for the work piece. He must also know how to use the various forming tools.

The hammersmith supervises the crew. Hammer Operators--operate huge presses equipped with either open or impression dies. This work differs from that of the hammersmith mainly because this operation shapes and forms hot metal by pressing or squeezing rather than by hammering. They must know how to regulate their machines, the proper heat of metal being formed, and how to set-up dies in the press. Upsetters--shape hot metal by applying pressure through the horizontal movement of one impression die against another. His duties require the aligning of dies, positioning metal stock between the dies, adjusting the required pressure, and proper heating of the metal stock. Heaters--must know how to adjust the furnace to obtain the temperature and atmosphere required. They read temperature gages and observe the color of the metal to determine when the correct temperature of the metal has been reached. They use tongs or mechanical equipment to transfer heated metal from the furnace to the hammer or press. Inspectors--check forgings for specifications as they relate to size, shape, and quality. This inspection may be done visually or with measuring instruments depending upon required accuracy. They also check forgings for strength and hardness with machines and testing devices. Diesinkers--are highly skilled craftsmen. They make the impression dies. Working from a blueprint or drawing, diesinkers form the shape of the die blocks with machine tools. EDM (electric discharge machining) and ECM (electrochemical machining) are new processes being used by sinkers to machine the dies today. In addition to these new processes, they must also be skillful in the use of hand tools, such as grinders and scrapers which are used to smooth and finish the die cavity.

Other forge shop workers clean and finish the forgings. These jobs include trimmers, grinders, sandblasting or shotblasting, picklers, and heat treaters.

Fig. 6-1. A gas fired forge. (Johnson Gas Appliance Co.)

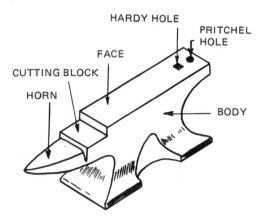

Fig. 6-2. The parts of an anvil.

THE FORGE

A forge is used to heat the metal to be shaped. It may be a gas or oil-fired furnace, or a coal forge, Fig. 6-1. To light a gas or oil furnace, place a lighted piece of paper in the fire box close to a burner. Turn on a small amount of air and then a little fuel until the furnace lights up. As the furnace heats up, turn on more fuel and air until the flame is blue. Too much air causes the formation of a heavy scale on the metal being forged. When you are through using a forge, close the gas and air valves.

ANVIL

Metal is hammered and bent into shape on an anvil, Fig. 6-2. The size of an anvil is determined by its weight. Commonly used sizes weigh from 150 lbs. to 300 lbs. A 100 to 200 lb. anvil is suitable for school use. Most anvils have either a cast steel, or cast iron body. The face is made of hardened steel welded to the body. It is smooth and should be kept free of dents and marks. The horn which is shaped like a cone is unhardened but tough. It is used for shaping rings, hooks, and curved parts. The cutting block which is located between the face and the horn, has a soft surface. It is used when cutting or chipping metal with a cold chisel--do not use the face for these operations. The hardy hole is square. It is used to hold square shank tools such as hardies, swages, and fullers, Fig. 6-3. The pritchel hole is used for bending small rods and punching holes in metal.

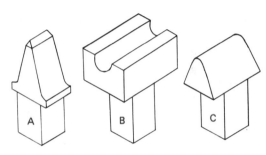

Fig. 6-3. Anvil tools. (A) Hardy to cut hot and cold metal; (B) Swage to smooth round stock (they are made in pairs--- the one that goes on top has a handle); (C) Fuller, to form depressions in heated metal (they are also made in pairs).

HAMMERS

Hammers and sledges of different types are used in hand forging, Fig. 6-4. The size of a hammer is given in ounces or pounds. The most common sizes found in school shops are: the ball peen, 6 oz. to 2 1/2 lbs., and the cross and straight peen blacksmith's hand hammers, 1 1/2 to 3 1/2 lbs. These hammers are usually made of forged steel, hardened, and given a polished finish.

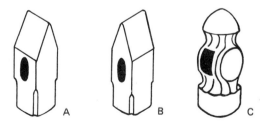

Fig. 6-4. Forging hammers. A—Cross peen; B—Straight peen; C—Ball peen.

FORGING PROCESSES

The metal must be heated to the correct temperature for shaping. Most mild steel should be heated to a good bright red. Thinner pieces of metal require less heat than thicker ones. Tool steel should be heated to a point between cherry red and orange. Never allow the metal to become so hot that sparks fly from it, since this causes the metal to oxidize and burn. Never hammer on tool steel after it loses the orange color and starts turning black since this will cause the metal to crack. All forging must be done at forging temperature, also with as few heatings as possible, because too much heating spoils the steel. Study each forging operation before starting, and have all the tools handy so when the metal is hot, hammering and forging can be done quickly.

HOLDING WORK

The metal to be forged must be held securely while it is being worked. A pair of tongs of suitable size and shape is used for this purpose. There are several sizes and shapes, but the most common are illustrated in Fig. 6-5. The straight-lip tongs that have a "V" notch in each jaw are used to hold square and round shapes, Fig. 6-5a. The other pair of straight-lip tongs is used to hold thin flat work, Fig. 6-5b. Single pick up tongs are designed for picking up either flat

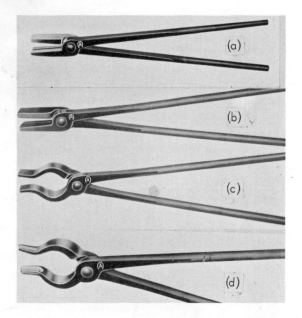

Fig. 6-5. Forging tongs: (A) Straight lip, with "V" notch in each jaw; (B) Straight lip; (C) Single pick up; (D) Curved lip, with fluted jaws. (Stanley Tools)

or round stock, Fig. 6-5c. The curved-lip tongs, with fluted jaws are used to hold bolts and irregular-shaped pieces, Fig. 6-5d. The jaws of the tongs must close evenly on the stock throughout their length, Fig. 6-6.

Fig. 6-6. Tongs gripping piece properly.

If tongs of suitable size are not available, slight adjustments can be made by heating and bending the jaws so that they close evenly on the stock.

UPSETTING METAL

The purpose of upsetting is to increase the thickness of the stock at a given point. This operation shortens the length of the piece so be sure to allow enough extra stock. To perform the upsetting operation, place the stock in the fire in a position that will heat the portion to be upset to a yellow heat. If the metal is long enough, pick it up with one hand and place the heated end on the face of the anvil, Fig. 6-7.

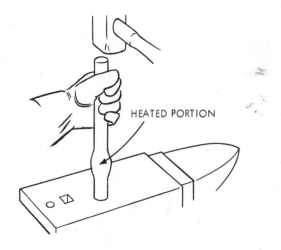

HEATED PORTION

Fig. 6-7. Upsetting a piece of metal.

Working rapidly, strike the cold end of the stock hard blows with a heavy hammer. If the stock bends, lay it flat on the anvil and straighten it with the hammer. Then continue the upsetting process until the desired thickness is obtained. If the stock becomes hard to work because of cooling, reheat it and continue the process. When the stock upsets too quickly at the end, dip it in water and proceed in the usual manner.

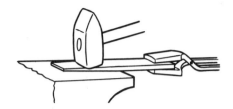

Fig. 6-8. Drawing out metal.

DRAWING OUT

In forging, drawing out stock means to lengthen the piece and to reduce a portion of it in size. The tapered part of a flat cold chisel is an example of drawing out metal. When forging mild steel, heat the portion to be worked to a bright yellow heat. Then quickly place the part to be drawn on the face of the anvil. Hold the piece firmly with tongs and strike the metal a few heavy blows, Fig. 6-8. Hold the hammer so that its face is parallel with the surface of the work piece when the blow is struck. Continue the drawing out process, rotating and striking the metal first on the broad face and then on the edge until the desired shape is obtained. While drawing out the metal each broad face should be hammered alternately. When drawing out metal to a round point as on a center punch, follow the steps shown in Fig. 6-9.

Fig. 6-9. Steps in forging the point of a center punch.

BENDING

To make a sharp bend, heat the stock at the point where the bend is to be made. Place the stock on the anvil face with the portion to be bent down at the

SAMMY SAFETY SAYS:

"Do not look into the opening of the furnace as the fuel is turned on. Do not operate the forge until your teacher shows you how.

Wear a face shield when hammering hot metal. The scale that flies is hot. Wear gloves when necessary and use tongs when handling hot metal. Wear an asbestos glove on the hand holding the stock. If the piece of metal is too short to hold by hand safely, grip it with tongs."

edge of the anvil. Strike the extended portion moderate blows with the hammer to bend the stock down to the desired angle, Fig. 6-10. Angular bends can also be made in the hardy hole or pritchel hole of the anvil. Bars can often be bent in a vise. Thin metal can be bent cold; heavy pieces must be heated.

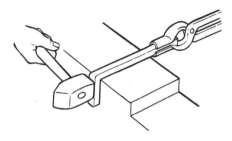

Fig. 6-10. Forging a sharp bend on the anvil.

FORMING AN EYE

Measure the length of metal it will take to make the eye, and mark the point with a prick punch. Heat the metal at this point, and bend it over the edge of the anvil to a 90 deg. angle, Fig. 6-11a. Heat and start bending the end to form the eye, Fig. 6-11b. Continue by heating and forming the eye over the anvil horn, Fig. 6-11c. Close the eye by holding it over the edge of the anvil, and striking it with a hammer, Fig. 6-11d.

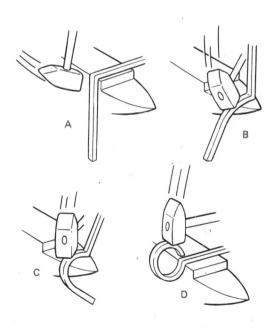

Fig. 6-11. Steps in forging an eye.

QUIZ — UNIT 6

1. What is forging?
2. What is the difference between production forging and the work of a blacksmith?
3. List the steps in lighting a gas forge.
4. What safety precautions should be followed when lighting the forge?
5. What are the parts of an anvil?

6. What is the proper heat for forging tool steel (as determined by color of metal)?
7. What is meant by drawing out metal?
8. What is the procedure for upsetting metal?
9. What are the steps for forming an eye?
10. List two safety precautions to be followed when doing hand forging.

In the school shop where there is danger of injury from flying metal chips, the importance of proper eye protection cannot be overemphasized.

WELDING

UNIT 7

1. **Career opportunities in the field of welding.**
2. **Welding with oxyacetylene equipment.**
3. **Types and preparation of welded joints.**
4. **Brazing metal.**
5. **Arc welding and spot welding.**

Welding is the process of joining metal pieces by heating them to the melting point, and allowing the molten portions to fuse or flow together. This process may be done with or without pressure. Industry uses welding to join parts together because it is an efficient, dependable, and practical process. The oldest form of welding is forge welding, which has been practiced by blacksmiths and other artisans for centuries. Today, industry is using many modern welding techniques that make it possible to join most any metal or alloy. Welding can be applied to practically all types of metal from large castings and huge structural shapes to the thinnest of sheet metals. In this unit we will study oxyacetylene, simple arc and spot welding processes.

CAREER OPPORTUNITIES

There are many jobs in the field of welding. With new welding techniques and wider use of welding processes, the number of jobs in this field will most probably increase. The principal employers are automobile manufacturers, aircraft plants, sheet metal fabricators, shipyards, steel mills, construction industries and repair shops. The earnings of highly skilled manual welders compare favorably with those of other skilled metalworking jobs. Flame-cutting and resistance welders who require little training, earn less than the skilled manual welders. Welding requires a steady hand, manual dexterity, and good eyesight. In addition to the development of skill in using welding equipment, the craftsman in this field of work must have a knowledge of blueprint reading, properties of metal, and planning procedures. A growing career in the welding field is the position of a welding technician. This job involves interpreting the engineer's plans, specifications, and being able to follow his instructions. As new and more sophisticated

welding processes are developed, technicians will be in great demand.

OXYACETYLENE WELDING

This welding process, usually called "gas welding," is done with a torch. The torch mixes oxygen and acetylene gases to provide fuel for the flame. This flame can be controlled to produce the heat required to melt and fuse the metals being joined. The flame burns at a temperature of over 6000 deg. F.

EQUIPMENT

Welding equipment, Fig. 7-1, includes two cylinders, one oxygen and one acetylene. These cylinders are equipped with regulators that can be adjusted to

Fig. 7-1. Oxygen and acetylene cylinders should be mounted vertically in a truck or chained to a post.

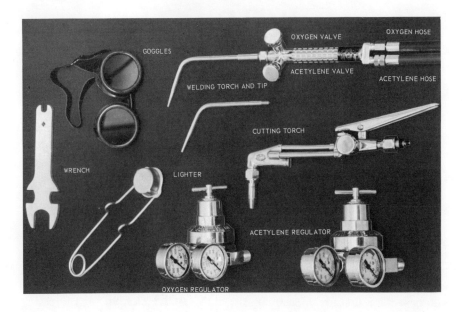

Fig. 7-2. Basic accessories for welding with oxyacetylene.

reduce the high cylinder pressures. Most regulators are equipped with two gages. One gage indicates the cylinder pressure and the other gage the amount of pressure in the hose. Two lengths of hose provide a means for carrying the gas from the cylinders to the welding torch which can be fitted with different size tips. To assist in identifying these hoses, they are color coded. The oxygen hose is green and the acetylene hose is red. Some of the basic accessories required for welding with oxyacetylene are shown in Fig. 7-2. In addition to those shown, fireproof gloves and a fireproof apron are needed.

TYPES AND PREPARATION OF JOINTS

Before welding you must decide which type of joint should be used for the job. The type of joint depends upon the kind of material, its thickness, and the nature of the job. To obtain a sound weld, the joint must be clean. Rust, scale, oil, and other impurities must be removed from the base metal.

Five basic types of joints that are common to both oxyacetylene and arc welding are: The butt joint, Fig. 7-3, Tee joint, Fig. 7-4, Lap joint, Fig. 7-5, Edge joint, Fig. 7-6, and Corner joint, Fig. 7-7.

The American Welding Society has established a set of standard welding symbols for these joints. These symbols are used by the draftsman to tell the welder what kind of weld should be made. Symbols indicate the exact specifications for welding operations to be done on the work piece. Before welding according to a blueprint or a drawing that has welding symbols on it, you should study the American Welding Society's Standard Welding Symbols publication.

ADJUSTING EQUIPMENT FOR WELDING

Check with your instructor before attempting to adjust the welding equipment. Adjusting the equipment for welding must be done properly to prevent damage to the gages and to observe safety precautions. Following is the recommended procedure:

SAMMY SAFETY
SAYS:

"Never play or get careless when using the welding equipment. Combustible gas and a fire must be handled carefully."

"Always wear welding goggles, fire-proof gloves, and fireproof apron when using welding equipment."

"Always use the spark lighter to light the torch — never use a match."

"Turn off the torch if it becomes necessary to change the position of work pieces or when you have completed the weld. Always hang the torch up carefully."

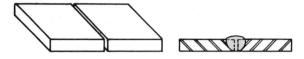

Fig. 7-3. Butt joint. Metal 1/8 in. thick can be welded from one side. Up to 3/8 in., weld joint on both sides. The joint must be beveled on thicker metal plate before welding.

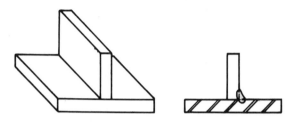

Fig. 7-4. Tee joint. Weld is made from one or both sides.

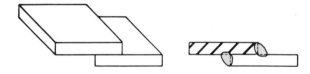

Fig. 7-5. Lap joint. Pieces to be welded should fit together tightly. A double weld is used when greater strength is needed.

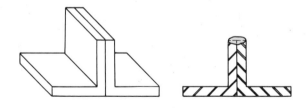

Fig. 7-6. Edge joint. This type joint is used where a great amount of strength is not needed. Generally the base metal serves as the filler metal.

1. Select the proper size tip for the job and carefully insert it in the torch. Refer to the chart furnished with the welding equipment for proper tip size. Be careful when tightening the tip to the torch so you do not strip the threads. Be sure the tip seats properly in the torch. If the tip needs cleaning, ask your instructor to give you the proper size tip cleaner.
2. Check the valves on the torch to be sure they are turned off (clockwise). Never close the valves too

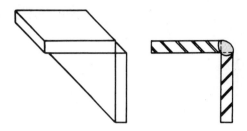

Fig. 7-7. Corner joint. Open corner joints are used when welding heavier plate. A light bead may be added to the inside to give the weld more strength.

tightly, just tight enough to prevent gas from leaking through.
3. Back-off the adjusting screws on both gages until they are loose. This prevents a sudden surge of excessive pressure on the gages. Do not remove the screws from the gages.
4. Using the cylinder wrench, open the acetylene cylinder valve 1/4 to 1/2 turn.
5. Open the oxygen cylinder valve slowly, continuing to turn the valve until it seats against the top of the valve.

LIGHTING THE TORCH

1. Open the acetylene valve on the torch and turn the acetylene regulator screw clockwise until the gage registers between five to eight pounds of pressure. Close torch valve.
2. Open the oxygen valve on the torch and repeat step number 1 for the oxygen. You will adjust the pressure differently for various size tips and welding jobs to be performed. Check the tip size and gas pressure chart prepared for the kind of welding equipment you are using.
3. The torch is ready to light. Put on the proper welding goggles and gloves.
4. Open the acetylene valve on the torch approximately 1/4 turn. Hold the torch with tip pointed away from the cylinders and your body. Light the torch with a flint lighter. NEVER USE A MATCH.
5. Quickly adjust the acetylene valve on the torch until the flame slightly extends from the end of

SAMMY SAFETY SAYS:

"When opening cylinder valves stand to one side of the regulator gages."

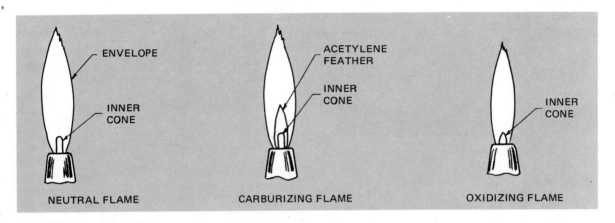

Fig. 7-8. Left. Neutral flame. The inner cone is smooth and rounded. Fig. 7-9. Center. A carburizing flame has three distinct flame sections. The inner cone is inside of another cone called acetylene feather. Fig. 7-10. Right. Oxidizing flame. The inner cone is sharp and pointed. The envelope is shorter.

the tip. Open the oxygen valve on the torch and adjust it to obtain the desired flame, Fig. 7-8. A neutral flame is best for most work. A carburizing flame, Fig. 7-9, is obtained when an excess of acetylene, which is indicated by streamers of acetylene (usually called feathers) comes from the inner cone. This kind of flame should not be used in fusion welding since it produces a brittle weld. An oxidizing flame, Fig. 7-10, is indicated by a hissing sound which is the result of too much oxygen. This kind of flame tends to burn the metal.

SHUTTING OFF THE EQUIPMENT

1. Close the torch acetylene valve first, then close the torch oxygen valve.
2. Close the acetylene cylinder valve first, then close the oxygen cylinder valve.
3. Open the torch acetylene valve to drain the gas from the regulator and hose.
4. Open the torch oxygen valve to drain the regulator and hose.
5. Turn out regulator screws on each regulator until they are loose to remove pressure from the diaphragms of the regulators.
6. Hang up the hose and torch. Do not put the torch or the hose over the cylinder regulators.

MAKING A PRACTICE WELD

Learning to weld takes considerable practice and experimentation. The quality of a finished weld is largely dependent upon the adjustment and manipulation of the flame. To see what effect the various flame adjustments have on a weld, make several practice runs on a piece of mild steel 3/16 in. thick by approximately 2 in. wide by 6 in. long.

1. Use a number 2 tip for this metal thickness. Place welding goggles on your forehead.
2. Put on welding gloves. Light the torch and adjust to a neutral flame.
3. Place the goggles over your eyes. Hold the inner cone of the flame about 1/8 in. above the piece of mild steel.
4. Hold the flame in one spot until a puddle 1/4 in. wide is formed. Keeping the puddle the same width, continue across the length of the practice piece of metal. Examine the results.
5. Adjust the torch to a carburizing flame. Run a bead parallel to the first bead about 1/2 in. over from it. Note the cloudy appearance of the molten puddle. Examine the results.
6. Adjust the torch to an oxidizing flame and run a bead parallel to the second bead about 1/2 in. over from it. Notice the violent agitation of the molten puddle. Examine the weld.
7. After the work piece has cooled, place it in a machinist's vise and bend it in the middle with a hammer. Examine the three welds. Note that the carburized bead may be cracked and the bead made with an oxidizing flame may have lost much of the scaled, oxidized material.
8. Take the work piece out of the vise and continue bending the metal until it is folded flat upon itself. The carburized and oxidized beads will probably be cracked while the bead made with a neutral flame bent as much as the original material without failure.

METAL THICKNESS	ROD SIZE (DIA)
18 gage	1/16 in.
1/16 in.	1/16 in. to 3/16 in.
1/8 in.	3/32 in. to 1/8 in.
3/16 in.	1/8 in. to 5/32 in.
1/4 in.	5/32 in. to 3/16 in.
3/8 in. and up	3/16 in. to 1/4 in.

Fig. 7-11. Recommended welding rod sizes for oxyacetylene welding. Mild steel welding rods are usually copper coated to prevent rusting. Cast-iron rods are square shaped. Brazing rods are made of brass or bonze. Mild steel and brazing rods are usually 36 in. long.

WELDING WITH FILLER ROD

After you have made the practice welds you should have a "feel" of the torch and control of the flame's distance from the work piece.

1. Prepare pieces of metal to be welded and arrange them in proper position on the welding table. Always wear proper goggles and gloves.
2. Select the proper size tip for the job and attach it to the torch.
3. Select the recommended rod size for the job. Check Fig. 7-11.
4. Set up the welding equipment and light the torch.
5. Adjust the torch for a neutral flame. Place the flame close to the joint. Move the torch in a small arc motion until the metal puddles (melts) and tacks together.
6. Using the same torch motion, start welding at the other end of the joint. Note: Steps 5 and 6 are very important. This keeps the joint of the two pieces being welded from spreading apart.
7. Add the filler rod to the joint as you weld. The rod should be moved in an arc opposite to the torch motion. Do not touch the torch tip with the rod. Keep the rod in the puddle. If the torch tip gets too close to the metal it will form small blow-holes in the weld and the torch may pop or backfire.
8. Develop a rhythm of torch and rod movement as you weld the joint. Also be careful to get good penetration as you fuse the rod and metal being welded.

BRAZING

Brazing is quite similar to soldering. An oxyacetylene welding torch is used to heat the metal until the brazing rod flows at the area being joined. The base metals are not melted. Joints that are properly brazed are very strong. A brazing rod, usually a copper alloy,

and a matching flux are used. Rods and fluxes may be purchased for work at various temperatures and different types of metals.

1. Parts to be brazed must be clean and free of impurities. Joints should make a good fit.
2. Adjust torch to a neutral flame and apply heat to the metals being joined until they are red hot. Heat the end of the brazing rod slightly and dip in the flux, causing it to cling to the rod.
3. Holding the rod just ahead of the flame, continue to heat the metal pieces until the brazing rod melts and flows on the pieces being brazed. If the brazing alloy balls up and solidifies, the joint is not hot enough.
4. After proper temperature has been reached, continue brazing across the joint. Keep your torch in motion to prevent hot spots. Avoid overheating which often causes a weak joint. A properly brazed joint will have a bright shiny color after the flux has been washed off with water.

ARC WELDING

Arc welding is the process of fusing metals using the heat of an electric arc. The high temperature of this arc (electric spark) melts the metal, forming a molten puddle. An electrode used to create the arc melts and serves as the filler rod for the joint. Arc welders are rated according to their current output in amperes. Fig. 7-12 shows the kind usually found in the average school shop.

Fig. 7-12. AC welding machine. (Hobart Brothers Co.)

WELDING

1. Prepare the joint and place it in the proper position. Clamps may be needed to hold the pieces in place.
2. Place the proper electrode in the holder and clamp the ground cable to the metal to be welded or to the metal table where the work piece is placed.
3. Adjust the welder to the correct amperage.
4. Arc welding gloves, apron, and sleeves should be worn to protect you from the intense light and heat to prevent burning your skin.
5. Put on a head shield, Fig. 7-13.

Fig. 7-13. Head shield for arc welding.
(Hobart Brothers Co.)

6. Turn the machine on and bring the electrode within a few inches of the work piece.
7. Drop the shield over your eyes and strike an arc. This is accomplished by striking the work piece with the electrode like you strike a match. Then raise the electrode slightly to form and maintain the arc. Keep the electrode moving while starting the arc to prevent it from sticking to the work piece.
8. After you have obtained the arc, keep the electrode within 1/16 to 1/8 in. of the metal being welded. As the electrode burns shorter, keep feeding it to the work piece to maintain the correct arc length.
9. The electrode is moved in a straight direction without a circular or weaving motion. When the job requires a wide joint, a weaving motion is used. In some cases it is necessary to run additional beads. Be sure you get almost 100 percent penetration in the weld. In all cases get the deepest penetration possible.

10. The correct welding speed is most important. Move the electrode along smoothly and evenly. You can determine the correct speed by examining the weld. Moving too slowly will produce too much excessive build-up of the weld. Moving too fast produces a shallow, uneven bead.
11. Clean the weld bead with a chipping hammer. Wear your safety goggles when chipping and wire brushing the weld. Handle the hot metal with a pair of tongs.

SAMMY SAFETY
SAYS:

"Never look at the arc with the naked eye. The arc can burn your eyes severely."

SPOT WELDING

This type of welding is a pressure-welding process called resistance welding. The weld is produced by heat generated by resistance to the flow of an electric current and by the application of pressure. Spot welding is used primarily in the fabrication of sheet metal. A filler metal is not needed. The weld is made between the metal pieces being joined.

Fig. 7-14. Portable spot welder unit.
(Miller Electric Mfg. Co.)

The spot welder, Fig. 7-14, is a portable hand operated machine. The machine has controls for regulating pressure, heat, and time cycle. The tips of the copper electrodes should be kept clean and properly shaped.

Spot welding is easy. If the proper procedure is used, the weld will be stronger than a rivet of equal diameter.

1. Clean the pieces of metal to be welded.
2. Turn on the electric power switch.
3. Clamp or hold the metal pieces together in the proper position and place the metal between the copper electrodes.
4. Apply pressure to the trigger or foot lever to make the weld. The pressure must be adjusted for different thicknesses of metal.
5. The correct weld time is very important. Spot welding machines are either controlled manually with the electric switch or they may have a built in timer which can be set.

QUIZ — UNIT 7

1. Welding is a process of joining metal pieces by _____.
2. Pieces of metal to be joined are heated at the point being welded to a temperature that _____ and _____ them together.
3. Name three principal employers of welders.
4. A growing career in the welding field is the position of welding _____.
5. The torch mixes _____ and _____ gases to provide fuel for the flame.
6. The flame burns at a temperature of over _____ deg. F.
7. The regulators used in oxyacetylene welding indicate _____ pressure and the amount of pressure in the _____.
8. Name the five basic types of joints common to both oxyacetylene and arc welding.
9. Who establishes the standard welding symbols that tell what kind of joint should be made?
10. What type of flame is best for most welding jobs?
11. If the torch tip gets too close to the metal being welded it will cause small _____ to form in the metal.
12. What size filler rod would you use when welding 18 gage metal?
13. When brazing, the base metals are not _____.
14. What is wrong if the brazing alloy balls up and solidifies on the pieces of metal being brazed?
15. Arc welding is a process of fusing metals with an _____.
16. Why shouldn't you look at the welding arc with the naked eye?
17. After the arc has been obtained, keep the electrode within _____ in. to _____ in. of the metal being welded.
18. Spot welding is a _____ welding process.
19. Spot welding is used mostly in the fabrication of _____.
20. When spot welding, the correct weld _____ is very important.

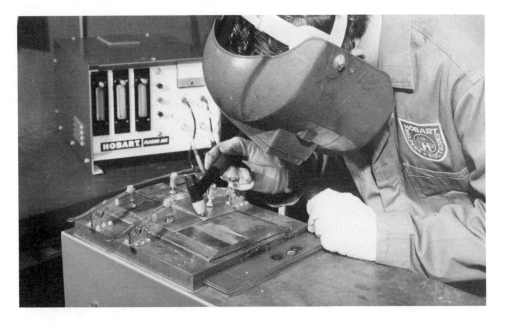

The new technological developments in the welding field, like this plasma arc welding, are increasing the demand for highly skilled technicians in the welding trades. (Hobart Brothers Co.)

HEAT TREATMENT OF STEELS

1. How to anneal, harden, and temper steel.
2. How to determine different temperatures by colors of heated metal.
3. How to caseharden low-carbon steel.

Heat treating is a process of heating and cooling steel in certain ways to change its properties. By properly heat treating, metals can be made harder and tougher. After you have made a cold chisel, center punch, screwdriver blade or any small tool, it will be necessary to heat treat it to make it useful. If the tip of a screwdriver blade, for example, is too hard it will be brittle and chip off when used. If the tip is too soft it will bend, so to be useful the tip of the blade must be heat treated. Tools must have a certain hardness, toughness, and brittleness to do their work. To obtain these characteristics there are four principal operations which may be performed to properly heat treat a piece of steel for its particular use. These operations are: Hardening, Tempering, Annealing and Casehardening.

HARDENING

Hardening is a process of heating steel to a certain temperature and then quenching (cooling) it in a suitable medium such as water, oil, or brine, depending upon the type of steel being hardened. Hardening is done in a furnace heated with oil, gas, electricity, or solid fuel. The steel is first heated to the desired temperature above the critical range in order to get the correct grain structure, and is then cooled quickly in a quenching medium in order to preserve this structure. Steel companies can supply information concerning temperatures and quenching procedures for their steels. This information is also given in Machinist's Handbooks. The temperature can be checked with a pyrometer attached to the furnace, a magnet, or by observing the color. A pyrometer, which is an electric thermometer, accurately registers the temperature in the furnace. Steel is magnetic until it reaches the critical temperature, then it is non-magnetic. When using this method, heat the metal

until the magnet stops picking it up. The metal should then be suddenly cooled. Determining the temperature by observing the color of the hot metal is not too accurate. However, the old time heat treater used this method for many years.

The hardness depends upon the amount of carbon in the steel, the temperature of the heated steel, and the speed of cooling.

TEMPERING

Tempering is a process which is used to remove a certain degree of hardness and brittleness of steel and increase its toughness. Tempering is also referred to as drawing the temper. Hardened steel breaks easily and is too hard and too brittle for many tools. Therefore, it is necessary to remove some of the hardness by softening the metal. Steel can be tempered using the color method as a guide to the proper temperature. The temper is gaged by the colors formed on the surface as the heat increases, Fig. 8-1. A modern method which is used when a quantity of pieces are to be tempered, is to place the hardened metal in a bath of molten lead, heated oil, or other liquids and heat them to the required temperature. The metal is

Degrees Fahrenheit	Colors For Tempering
440	Yellow
460	Straw-yellow
470	Straw
500	Brown
520	Brown-purple
540	Purple
570	Blue

Fig. 8-1. Colors for tempering.

then removed from the bath and quenched. The bath method does a more uniform job of tempering, and the temperature can be held to close limits.

ANNEALING

Annealing is the opposite of hardening. It is a process of softening steel to make it easier to machine, cut, stamp, or shape, and to relieve stresses and hardness resulting from cold working. In annealing, the metal is cooled as slowly as possible. The slower the cooling, the softer it is when cold. To anneal steel, heat it slowly to the critical temperature. Cool it slowly by packing it in hot ashes to keep the air away, or it may be cooled off with the furnace.

CASEHARDENING

Casehardening is the hardening of the outer surface of metal. Only low-carbon steel and wrought iron can be casehardened. This process adds a small amount of carbon to the case (outside) of the metal part so it can be heat treated and made hard. The center, or core of the metal remains soft. Casehardening is done to parts which need a hard wearing surface such as gears, screws, hand tools, and roller bearings. Industry uses several methods to caseharden parts. Cyaniding is a common one and is done by placing the metal in a bath of molten cyanide. This method is too dangerous however for school shops. Carburizing is another method. This work is placed in a metal box containing a mixture of bone, leather,

charcoal, and carburizing materials. The container is then sealed and heated to about 1650 deg. F so the piece soaks up the carbon and forms a high carbon case on the outside. The piece is cooled in the carburizing box. Take the piece out of the container, reheat it to the critical temperature and quench.

HEAT TREATING PROCEDURE

Many of the projects made in the school shop require heat treatment. Cold chisels, center punches, hammer heads, and small parts can be heat treated very successfully with inexpensive equipment. The source of heat can be a small gas or oil-fired furnace, Fig. 8-2, blowtorch, forge, gas welding torch, or a bench soldering furnace. The quenching bath can be a pail of water, tempering oil, or brine, depending on the type of metal. Forging tongs can be used to hold the hot metal.

The tool steel used in most school shops is a water-hardening type. It is generally in an annealed state ready for cutting, drilling, filing, or machining. If it becomes necessary to heat the metal for certain operations, you will have to anneal it again if more cutting or shaping has to be performed. Annealing, hardening, and tempering operations may occur as a series of steps in the heat treatment operations, or annealing may be a separate process to remove internal strain developed while the metal is worked. Hardening may be done without performing either of the other processes. Tempering always follows annealing and hardening. Following is the procedure you may use to heat treat shop projects:

ANNEALING

1. After the piece has been forged to shape, heat it throughout the portion to be annealed. A moderate flame should be used if gas is the source of heat.
2. Turn the metal as it is heated until it reaches a cherry red or the color just below the critical range of the steel being annealed.
3. Remove the metal from the heat and cover it immediately with pulverized coke or air slaked lime. Keep the metal covered until it is cold.

HARDENING

1. Heat the metal to its critical temperature. For example, .70 to .90 carbon, water-hardening, tool steel is heated to about 1450-1550 deg. F. The

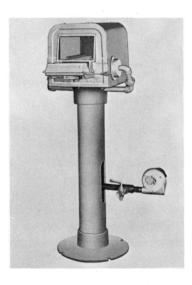

Fig. 8-2. A gas fired heat treating furnace that will reach 2300 deg. (Johnson Gas Appliance Co.)

Deg. F	
752	Red heat (visible in the dark)
975	Red heat (visible in the daylight)
1292	Dark red
1472	Dull cherry red
1652	Cherry red
1832	Bright cherry red
2190	Lemon yellow
2300	White
2500	Welding heat (sparks fly)

Fig. 8-3. Colors for judging high temperature.

Deg. F	Color	Tools
430	Pale yellow	Hammer faces, Scribers, Scrapers
460	Straw yellow	Center punches
500	Brown	Cold chisels
540	Purple	Screwdrivers

Fig. 8-5. Tempering colors for common tools.

color closest to this temperature is a cherry red to a bright red, Fig. 8-3. Be sure to have the metal heated uniformly.

2. Quench the metal quickly in the correct cooling solution. Whirl the metal around in the solution so it will cool quickly and evenly, Fig. 8-4. Water is

Fig. 8-4. Quenching heated steel. Whirl the metal in a circular motion, with a slight up and down movement at the same time.

used for most tool steels. The temperature of the water should be between 60 to 80 deg. F.

3. Check the metal for hardness by running a new file across a corner or edge. If the metal is hard, the file will not cut in.

TEMPERING

The entire piece of metal can be tempered by heating it in a furnace to the temperature which will produce the degree of toughness and hardness desired, Fig. 8-5. Remove the piece and cool it quickly in the correct quenching solution.

To draw the temper on small tools such as center punches, screwdriver blades, or cold chisels, the following procedure may be used:

1. Harden the entire tool.
2. Polish about one inch of the surface at the cutting edge or point with abrasive cloth. This will make it easier for you to see the change of colors as the heat travels toward the point or cutting edge of the tool.
3. Heat the metal slowly and uniformly back of the polished surface. Watch carefully for the colors as they travel toward the hardened end. The colors generally appear in the following order--pale yellow, straw color, light brown, light purple, blue-red, blue, and finally gray.
4. When the proper color appears at the cutting edge or point, plunge the metal into the quenching solution quickly, and move it in a circular motion until completely cooled.
5. Check the tool for hardness by using it on a scrap piece of metal. If the piece chips, it is too hard and must be heated to a color of a slightly lower degree of hardness and cooled as before. If the point or edge bends under practical use, it is too soft and must be hardened and tempered again.

The Sand Box method is another way which can be used to temper small pieces. This is done by placing the hardened tool (polished as described in Step 2) in the sand with the point sticking out. Heat the sand in the bottom of the metal box. Watch the temper colors as they travel toward the point. When the correct color reaches the point, remove the tool with tongs and cool it quickly.

Hardening and tempering may be performed with one heat. This is done by heating the metal to the proper tempering temperature. Remove the tool from the heat, and quickly clean the point with abrasive cloth. Then insert the tool in the cooling solution and remove it quickly. Watch the colors carefully as they appear. When the proper color appears at the work end, quickly plunge the tool in the cooling solution and move it around in a circular motion, with a slight up and down motion. The up-and-down motion helps prevent fractures or checks at the line where the tool is placed in the cooling solution.

CASEHARDENING

1. Place the pieces to be casehardened in metal boxes or pipes.
2. Pour Kasenite (a non-poisonous commercial compound) around them. Be sure the pieces are completely surrounded with the compound.
3. Place the lid on the box and put it in the furnace.
4. Heat the box to about 1650 deg. F. The depth of casehardening will depend upon the length of time the part is kept hot. A depth of approximately 1/32 in. is obtained if the packed metal is held at the above temperature for about four hours.
5. Remove the box from the furnace and allow it to cool.
6. Reheat the parts to about 1600 deg. F and quench in water. This will give the metal a hardened case and leave the core soft.

SAMMY SAFETY
SAYS:

"When working with hot metal be careful not to burn yourself or another person. Always wear protective clothing."

Simple casehardening can be done by heating the metal to a bright red and placing it in a container filled with a commercial hardening compound. Roll or move the metal around in the compound. The compound will melt and adhere to the surface of the metal, forming a hard coating of steel around it. Reheat the metal to a bright red color and plunge it into clean, cold water. If a deeper case is desired, repeat the above steps.

The heat treating process is highly scientific and procedures vary with the many kinds of metals being used in industry. The heat treater must have a knowledge of chemistry and physics. Industries where foundry, forging, and machining of metal is done require the services of skilled heat treaters. Today most of the heat treating is automated; however, the technicians, engineers, and inspectors are responsible for obtaining the correct metal characteristics with the automatic equipment.

QUIZ — UNIT 8

1. Why is it necessary to heat treat a cold chisel?
2. List the three characteristics tools should have to do their work.
3. How is tool steel hardened?
4. Describe one method for drawing the temper on a center punch.
5. Three cooling solutions are _____, _____ and _____.
6. Steel is magnetic until it reaches the _____ temperature.
7. Tempering tool steel removes a certain degree of _____ and _____.
8. Why does hardened steel have to be tempered for many tools?
9. Describe how tool steel is annealed.
10. Tempering always follows _____ and _____.
11. Why should the metal be moved in a circular motion in the cooling solution?
12. Can hardening and tempering be performed with one heat?
13. What is casehardening?
14. Are all steels of the water-hardening type?
15. The pack method of carburizing is a method used to _____ metal.

FOUNDRY

1. Principal methods of casting metal.
2. Some of the characteristics of a good pattern.
3. How to make a core.
4. How to make a sand mold.

The foundry process is a vital link in the chain of metal industries. Most of the metal products we use every day contain some cast parts. The automobile, bicycle, refrigerator, plumbing fixtures, and many other items around the home have foundry made parts. Founding is a process of producing metal objects by pouring molten metal into a hollow mold made usually of sand. Articles produced by founding are called castings.

CAREER OPPORTUNITIES

Founding provides many jobs for laborers, semi-skilled workers, skilled workers, technicians, and engineers. The engineer and the metallurgist are responsible for controlling the quality of the metal required for the objects to be cast. Highly skilled woodworkers and metalworkers, called pattern-makers, make the patterns. Molders ram up the molds. Coremakers are a specialized group of workers who make the cores. The melter operates the furnace which melts the metal and the metal is poured into the molds by the pourer. Chippers, grinders, and finishers clean up the castings.

METHOD OF CASTING

Green sand casting is a method generally used in school shops. A material, consisting of a mixture of sand and clay is rammed into a mold. Molten metal is poured into a cavity formed in the sand mold. After the metal has solidified, the molds are broken up and the sand is used for another mold.

Permanent molds are used for producing large quantities of identical pieces. These molds are made of steel and used primarily for casting nonferrous metals such as aluminum, brass, and bronze.

Investment casting, which is sometimes referred to as lost wax casting, is used for casting jewelry, dental structures and parts requiring very close tolerances. In the process a wax pattern is coated with an invest-ment powder which hardens forming a shell around the wax. The wax is then melted out leaving a cavity into which the molten metal is poured.

Die casting is a method of casting nonferrous metals in which the molten metal is forced into a steel mold or die under pressure. Castings can be made quickly and economically on automatic ma-chines by this method. Die castings can be produced with finer finish, detail, and greater accuracy than ordinary sand castings.

A foundry in the school shop provides a means for making many interesting projects such as wall plaques, ash trays, lamps, candlestick holders, parts for home workshop tools, and machines to mention a few. By using a little imagination and creative ability, you will be able to design and make some very useful projects in this area.

PATTERNMAKING

Patterns are needed to form the cavity in the sand mold into which molten metal is poured. They may be made of wood, metal, plaster of Paris, or wax. A metal pattern lasts longer and keeps its shape better. Metals commonly used are aluminum, cast iron, steel, and brass. Woods generally used for patterns are white pine, mahogany, cherry, maple, birch, and fir. White pine is usually preferred because it works easily, is readily glued, and is reasonably durable. Wood patterns should be varnished to protect them against moisture. Coloring powders can be added to the varnish to identify various parts of the pattern.

You can probably find many articles around your home which may be used as patterns for foundry work. Small trays, plaques, paper weights, book ends, etc. make good patterns providing they have enough draft to be pulled.

Draft refers to the taper on a pattern that makes it possible to remove it easily from the sand mold, Fig. 9-1. If a pattern does not have enough draft, the mold will break when the pattern is pulled. As a general rule each side should be tapered 1/8 in. for each foot of surface to be drawn. Fillets are used in sharp internal angles, Fig. 9-1. These fillets can be made of wax, leather, or wood.

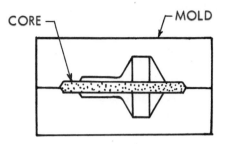

Fig. 9-2. Core in mold.

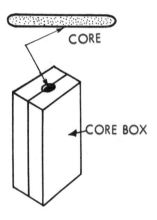

Fig. 9-3. Core box.

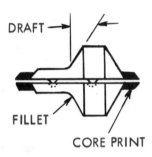

Fig. 9-1. Split pattern.

Metal takes up more space when it is hot than when it is cold. Therefore, the pattern must be made larger to allow for this shrinkage. For example, cast iron shrinks about 1/8 in. to the foot, so the rule in reality would be 12 1/8 in. long. The additional length is gradually gained in the length of the rule. The shrinkage allowance varies with the kind of metal being cast, and the size and shape of the casting. To compensate for this contraction of the castings in cooling, the following allowances are made: cast iron 1/8 in. per ft., yellow brass 7/32 in. per ft., aluminum 1/8 to 5/32 in. per ft. If the cast piece is to be machined, the pattern should be large enough to produce a piece that can be cleaned by leaving no rough spots or flaws after it has been cut to size.

CORES

A core is used in molding to form a hole or hollow space in a casting, Fig. 9-2. Cores are made from washed silica sand and a bonding material. The sand and binder is mixed until the binder is uniformly distributed in the sand. The core sand is molded to shape in a core box, Fig. 9-3. Core prints are provided

on patterns to form recesses in the mold to support the core, Fig. 9-1. The core is then turned out onto a plate and baked in an oven. The oven temperature and baking time depends on the size of the core and the kind of binder used. The temperature and baking time should be controlled to produce a core with enough hardness and strength to withstand the flow of the molten metal as it is poured into the mold cavity around the core. Wires can be embedded in large cores to provide additional strength in sections requiring greater strength. Large cores should be vented to permit passage of mold gases. If the core has two or more parts that are to be assembled, they can be bonded together with a flour paste. To improve the surface smoothness, coat the core with a wash of either talc or graphite.

MAKING A SAND MOLD

1. Prepare the molding sand by mixing and tempering. To temper the sand, sprinkle it with a little water and mix with a shovel, until all the lumps have been removed. The sand is properly tempered if a lump squeezed in your hand remains in

a lump, retains the sharp impressions of your fingers, and leaves the hand clean. When the lump is broken it should break with clean, square edges. If the sand sticks to your hand it is too wet. <u>Properly tempered sand is necessary to get good castings</u>. If the sand is too damp when the melted metal is poured into the mold, steam will form faster than it can escape through the pores of the sand.

2. Place the drag half of the flask on a molding board with the pins pointing down, Fig. 9-4.

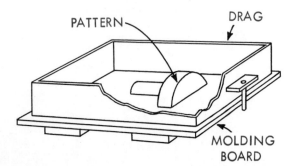

Fig. 9-4. Pattern and drag placed on molding board.

Place the pattern in the center with its flat side down on the board. Dust the pattern with just enough parting compound to cover its surface.

3. Set the riddle on top of the drag and fill it with sand. Riddle the sand over the pattern until it is covered 1 in. or more, Fig. 9-5.

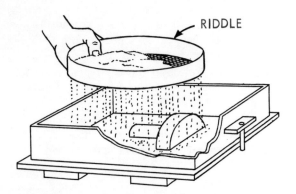

Fig. 9-5. Riddling molding sand over pattern.

4. Pour the rest of the sand left in the riddle into the drag. Shovel in more sand until the drag is heaping full.

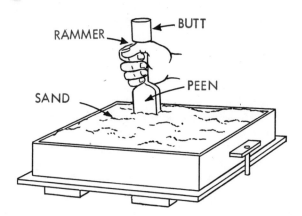

Fig. 9-6. Ramming the sand down in the drag and around the pattern.

5. Press the sand down in the drag and around the pattern with the peen end (small end) of the rammer, Fig. 9-6. The large end of the rammer is the butt. Be careful not to strike the pattern, or the edges of the drag. Ram the sand in firmly around the pattern and drag with the butt end. Properly ramming the sand is very important. If it is not rammed enough the sand may not be packed around the pattern firmly enough to give a good, sharp impression. If the sand is rammed too tightly the pores will not be large enough to allow the hot gasses formed in the mold to escape.

6. Strike off the excess sand on the top of the mold with a strike bar, Fig. 9-7. Sprinkle a handful of

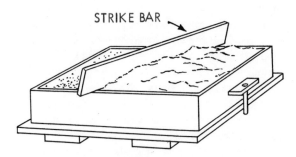

Fig. 9-7. Striking off excess sand with the strike bar.

sand over the mold and lay a bottom board on the top. Move the bottom board back and forth, pressing down at the same time, until it sets firmly against the edges of the drag.

7. Holding the mold board, drag, and bottom board

firmly, carefully roll the drag over. The pins are now pointing up, the bottom board is at the bottom and the molding board is on top.

8. Remove the molding board. The flat side of the pattern is now visible. Check the surface of the sand and smooth with the slick, spoon, trowel, and lifter if necessary, Fig. 9-8. Also be sure the

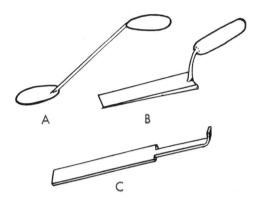

Fig. 9-8. Molders tools. (A) Slick and spoon; (B) Trowel; (C) Lifter.

sand is packed around the edges of the pattern. Carefully blow off any extra particles of sand.

9. Dust some parting compound over the pattern, and sand to keep the two halves from sticking together. Set the cope part of the flask on the drag, Fig. 9-9. Insert the sprue pin and riser pin.

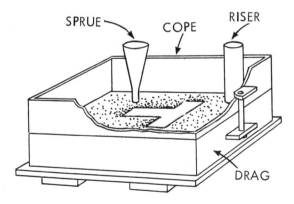

Fig. 9-9. Cope set on drag with riser pin and sprue pin in place.

The sprue pin is a tapered wooden or metal pin that is used to make a hole in the cope through which the metal is poured into the mold. The

riser which has no taper, is used to make a hole for the metal to rise in and make up for some of the shrinkage when the metal cools.

10. Riddle sand into the cope, and ram as in Steps 3, 4, 5, and 6.

11. Vent the mold over the pattern so air, steam, and gas can escape as the molten metal is poured into the mold. This will help prevent the mold from exploding and keep blow holes (holes made by bubbles) from forming in the casting. A 1/16 in. welding rod slightly pointed on one end makes an excellent vent rod. Do not damage the pattern. A safe method is to push the vent rod into the mold slowly until it touches the pattern, and then pull it back about 1/4 in. Grip the vent rod at this level with your fingers. Punch several holes in the mold over the pattern, being careful to stop when the tips of your fingers touch the sand.

12. Remove the sprue pin and the rise pin. Shape the top of the sprue hole like a funnel, with your fingers. Be sure there is no loose sand around the sprue and riser holes.

13. Lift the cope section of the flask off and lay it on its edge. Carefully moisten the sand around the pattern with a camel's hair brush or wet bulb. This makes the sand around the pattern firmer, and keeps the mold from breaking when the pattern is removed.

14. Place a draw pin in the pattern. If the pattern is metal the draw pin has threads on one end that are screwed into a tapped hole in the pattern. A sharp pointed spike or a large wood screw may be used as a draw pin to remove a wood pattern. Rap the draw pin on all sides until the pattern is completely loose in the sand. Carefully and with a steady pull, lift the pattern straight up from the mold. If there is a little breaking off of the sand, repair it with a molder's tool.

15. Cut a small gate (channel) in the sand of the drag from the cavity made by the pattern to the place where the sprue is located. The width and depth of the gate will vary according to the size of the casting. The larger the casting, the larger the gate. For small plaques or book-ends, the gates should be about 1/2 in. deep and 1 in. wide. A piece of sheet metal 3 in. square, bent into a U-shape,

SAMMY SAFETY SAYS:

"Do not get the sand too wet. Water is an enemy of molten metal."

makes an excellent gate cutter. Cut away a little sand at a time until the gate is completed. Now cut a gate between the riser and the cavity. Patch up any small breaks that have occurred in the mold. Blow off all loose sand with the bellows. <u>It is extremely important that all particles of loose sand are removed from the gates and cavity.</u> Small particles of sand in the mold will cause the casting to have pinholes.

16. Carefully replace the cope section on the drag. Check to be sure the mold is completely closed. Place a flask weight on top of the mold to keep the molten metal from lifting up the sand. Set the mold on the floor. It is now ready to receive the melted metal.

To make a mold with a split pattern, follow the same steps as described above except that half of the pattern is rammed up first in the drag. After the molding board is removed the other half of the pattern is put in place on the half in the drag. The cope section of the flask is put in place and the steps described are followed. When molding a split pattern, the largest half of the pattern should be rammed up in the drag.

MELTING FURNACE

There are several kinds of furnaces for melting metal. Commercial foundries use cupola furnaces to melt large amounts of metal. In a school shop where only a small amount of casting is done a small melting furnace is used such as shown in Fig. 9-10. This furnace will melt aluminum, brass, and other light metals. Lead, tin, and some alloys can be melted in a large soldering furnace, forge, or with a gas welding torch. However, a melting furnace and a crucible is the safest and best method. The crucible can be used as the pouring ladle. Lifting tongs are used to pick up the crucible and place it in the crucible shank for pouring. Fig. 9-11, gives the melting points of common metals.

Metal	Degrees Fahrenheit
Solder (50/50)	400
Pewter	420
Tin	449
Lead	621
Zinc	787
Aluminum	1218
Brass	1700
Silver	1761
Copper	1981

Fig. 9-11. Melting points of metals.

POURING THE METAL

1. Select a crucible which is large enough to hold enough metal to fill the cavity, sprues, and risers. Fill the crucible with the pieces of metal to be melted.
2. Place the crucible in the furnace. Light the furnace and heat until the metal reaches the pouring temperature. Do not overheat. Overheated metal will produce defective castings.
3. Turn the furnace off. First turn off the air, then the gas. Add flux (commercial fluxes are used for aluminum, brass, and other alloys) to purify the

Fig. 9-10. Melting furnace.
(Johnson Gas Appliance Co.)

SAMMY SAFETY
SAYS:

"Dress properly when working with molten metal. Wear a pair of clear goggles, leggings, and asbestos gloves.
Never stand or look over the mold during the pouring or immediately after the pouring because the molten metal might spurt out of the mold.
Do not light the furnace until you have your teacher's permission. If cold metal must be added to melted metal, be sure it is perfectly dry, and that tongs used are also perfectly dry, or an explosion will result."

metal. Stir the metal to bring the impurities to the top. Skim off the impurities (called slag).

4. Remove the crucible from the furnace with the crucible tongs, and place it in the crucible shank. Pick up the crucible shank so you are in a comfortable position. Stand to one side of the mold and pour the metal as quickly as possible into the mold in a steady stream. It must be poured rapidly enough to keep the gate and sprue full until the mold is filled.

5. After the metal has cooled, shake out the mold and remove the casting. The casting may still be hot so handle it with tongs.

QUIZ — UNIT 9

1. List four jobs in commercial foundry work and describe each one.
2. List the principal methods of casting metal.
3. Name five kinds of wood used for pattern-making.
4. What is meant by "draft?"
5. Give two reasons why pattern must be larger than finished casting.
6. What is the purpose of a core?
7. What is the purpose of "core prints?"
8. What is a flask?
9. What is the difference between the drag and the cope?
10. How is molding sand tempered?
11. Describe the purpose of the riser and the sprue.
12. What is the purpose of the gate?
13. Why is parting compound dusted on the pattern?
14. How should you be dressed when pouring molten metal?
15. Why is water an enemy of molten metal?

Overhead crane moves crucible of molten aluminum which has just been tapped from the electrolytic cells, or pots, in this potline. (Kaiser Aluminum & Chemical Corp.)

MACHINE SHOP

1. **Using measuring tools to take accurate measurements.**
2. **Machining metal on the lathe.**
3. **Information about the metal shaper and milling machine.**

The machine shop plays an important role in the field of industry. Machine tools cut and shape metal more rapidly and more accurately than can be done by hand. The progress of industrial manufacturing and mass production depend upon machine tools. A skillful craftsman in metalwork should acquire an understanding of machine shop processes, and particularly the ability to work with accuracy and close tolerances.

CAREER OPPORTUNITIES

There are many opportunities in the machining occupations for the bright and ambitious person. A skilled machinist is always in demand. There are thousands of craftsmen employed in skilled and semi-skilled machining occupations which include machine tool operators, all-round machinists, tool and diemakers, set up men, and layout men. The tool and diemaker is a highly skilled craftsman in the metalworking field. He must be able to operate machine tools and use precision measuring instruments. Other requirements include a knowledge of mathematics, blueprint reading, and machine operations.

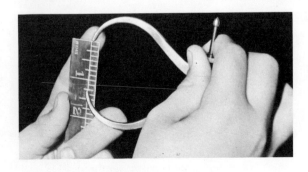

Fig. 10-1. Setting an outside caliper.

MEASURING TOOLS

Measuring carefully and accurately is essential to good machine work. As a beginning machine shop student, you will want to learn to take accurate measurements with some of the basic devices used by the machinist. Some information on measuring tools was given in Unit 4. In this Unit we will discuss Inside and Outside Calipers, and the Micrometer.

OUTSIDE CALIPER

This tool is used to take external measurements of cylindrical stock. To set an outside caliper, hold the instrument in the right hand and a scale in the left hand, Fig. 10-1. One leg of the caliper is supported against the end of the scale with a finger. Adjust the other leg until it splits the line on the scale which represents the correct measurement. To take a measurement, hold the caliper at right angles to the center line of the work and push it gently back and forth across the diameter of the cylinder to be measured, Fig. 10-2. The caliper is properly adjusted when it will slip over the piece with a very slight drag. Do not force the caliper over the work since this will spring the legs and the measurement will not be accurate.

INSIDE CALIPER

An inside caliper is used to gage inside diameters. To set an inside caliper for a desired dimension, hold a scale square on a flat surface. Then rest one leg of the tool on this surface at the edge and end of the scale. Adjust the other leg until it centers the proper graduation on the scale, Fig. 10-3. To take a measurement with an inside caliper, place it in the hole as indicated in Fig. 10-4. Adjust the caliper until

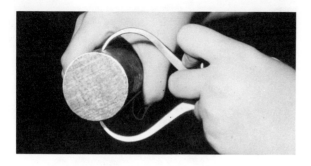

Fig. 10-2. Taking a measurement with an outside caliper.

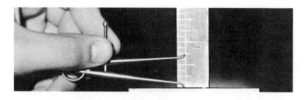

Fig. 10-3. Setting an inside caliper.

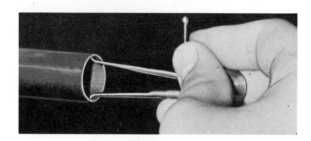

Fig. 10-4. Taking a measurement with an inside caliper.

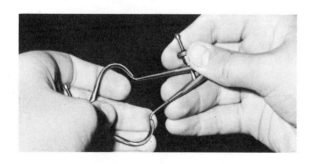

Fig. 10-5. Transferring measurements.

caliper, Fig. 10-5. Pivot the top point of the inside caliper in and out of the top point of the outside caliper. Adjust the thumb screw until the leg drags slightly as it contacts the leg of the outside caliper.

MICROMETER

A micrometer is a precision measuring tool which is used by the machinist. He calls it a "mike." Micrometers are made in different sizes and styles. The outside mike which will be described in this unit resembles a C clamp, Fig. 10-6. It has 40 threads per

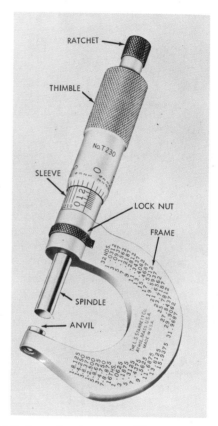

Fig. 10-6. Parts of a micrometer. (The L. S. Starrett Co.)

inch on the screw. One complete turn of the thimble moves the spindle 1/40 in. or 0.025 in. The thimble is marked off in 25 equal parts, each of which is 1/1000 in. or 0.001. On the sleeve there are 40 lines to the inch. Every four divisions on the sleeve are marked 1, 2, 3, etc., which represents 0.100, 0.200, 0.300 in., etc.

READING THE MICROMETER

1. Turn the thimble until the spindle is closed against the anvil. The reading should be zero with

it will slip into the hole with a very slight drag. To transfer measurements from an inside caliper to an outside caliper or vice versa, rest the point of one leg of the inside caliper on the point of an outside

the 0 mark on the thimble directly over the 0 mark on the sleeve.

2. Back off the thimble slowly. As each mark on the thimble passes the horizontal line on the sleeve the micrometer has been opened 0.001 in. When the thimble has been backed off one complete turn, 25 of these marks have passed the horizontal line on the sleeve and the micrometer has been opened 0.025 in.

3. To read the micrometer, first take the reading on the sleeve and then add to it the reading on the thimble. For example in Fig. 10-7, you can see

Fig. 10-9. Taking a measurement with a micrometer.

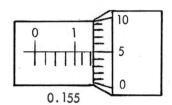

Fig. 10-7. One hundred fifty-five thousandths of an inch (0.155).

two divisions past the 1 on the sleeve, or six full divisions. The thimble reading is 5. Your reading would be 0.155 in. (0.025 in. x 6 = 0.150 in. + .005 in. = 0.155 in.) Study Fig. 10-8 and see if you can read the micrometer settings.

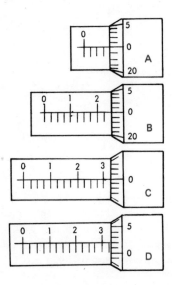

Fig. 10-8. "Mike" readings. (A) One hundred thousandths of an inch (0.100); (B) Two hundred fifty thousandths of an inch (0.250); (C) Three hundred twenty-five thousandths of an inch (0.325); (D) Three hundred twenty-seven thousandths of an inch (0.327).

After you learn to read the mike, practice using it by measuring some pieces of stock. When using the mike, hold it in the right hand and screw the thimble down until it lightly touches the stock, Fig. 10-9. Be careful not to screw it down too tight. Take the reading. Back the spindle off the stock and remove the mike and put it in a safe, clean place. Do not mike a piece of metal while it is turning in the lathe. Never tap a micrometer against other objects or drop it, since this may destroy its accuracy.

THE METAL LATHE

A metal lathe is used to cut and shape metal by revolving the piece against a cutting tool which is clamped on a movable carriage mounted on the lathe bed. They are used to perform many processes, including turning down metal rods, facing, cutting off, turning tapered sections, cutting threads, drilling, and boring.

The principal parts of the lathe include the heatstock, tailstock, bed, carriage, and the feeding and threading mechanisms, Fig. 10-10. After you become familiar with the names and location of the various parts of the lathe, get permission from your teacher to move the different handles and levers by hand, with the power off, to see what they do. All parts should move easily, never force them.

TURNING BETWEEN CENTERS

1. Carefully locate the center on both ends of the stock to be turned. The center of round stock may be located using the centerhead of the combination set, Fig. 10-11. Rectangular and square pieces are easily centered by drawing diagonal lines, Fig. 10-12.

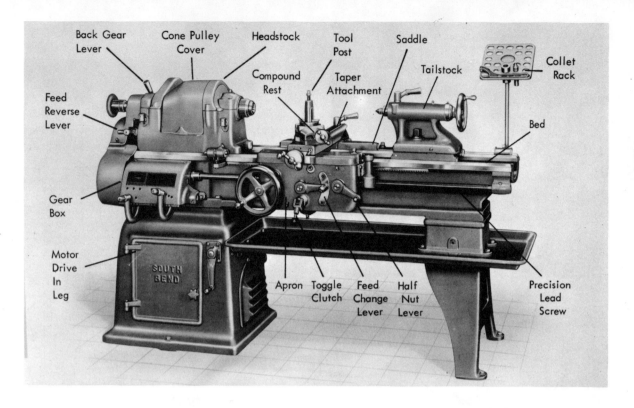

Fig. 10-10. Principal parts of a metal lathe.   (South Bend Lathe)

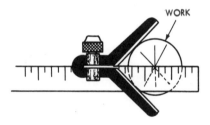

Fig. 10-11. Locating the center of round stock.

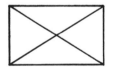

Fig. 10-12. Locating the center of square and
rectangular stock.

2. Center punch the center point on each end of the
stock.
3. Check the alignment of the lathe centers, Fig.
10-13. The live center should run true. Carefully
bring the dead center to within 1/16 in. of the
live center. If the points of the two centers are
not in line, move the tailstock over by adjusting
the setover screws, Fig. 10-14.

4. Remove live center and replace it with a drill
chuck, Fig. 10-15. Fasten a combination drill and
countersink in the chuck, Fig. 10-16.

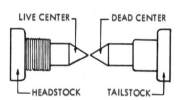

Fig. 10-13. Checking alignment of lathe centers, looking
from above.

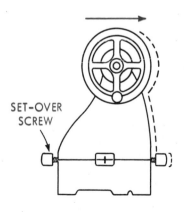

Fig. 10-14. Setting tailstock.

7. Apply lard, oil or cutting compound to drill when drilling steel. Cast iron should be drilled dry.

8. Hold the work with the left hand and start the lathe and feed by turning the tailstock spindle handwheel slowly until the center hole is drilled to the correct size, Fig. 10-18. Reverse the work

Fig. 10-18. Center drilled holes. (A) Properly drilled; (B) Drilled too deep.

Fig. 10-15. Remove live center from headstock with a knockout rod. Hold the center so it will not fall and damage the point.

Fig. 10-16. A combination drill and countersink. (Cleveland Twist Drill Co.)

5. Move the tailstock to such a position that the work just fits between the point of the drill and the dead center, and clamp the tailstock in place.

6. Put the center punch mark of one end of the stock on the drill point. Holding the work piece steady, turn the tailstock wheel to bring the dead center into the other center punch mark carefully, Fig. 10-17.

in the lathe and drill the other end.

9. Remove the drill chuck and screw a faceplate on the headstock spindle. Clean and oil the threads of the headstock spindle and faceplate. Place a board across the ways of the lathe and screw the faceplate onto the spindle until it is tight against the shoulder. Never bring the faceplate against the spindle shoulder with a bang since this will make it difficult to remove.

10. Clean out the spindle hole with a rag and insert the live center.

11. Clamp the smallest size lathe dog that will fit on one end of the work piece.

12. Place a small amount of white lead lubricant in the center hole at the tailstock end. Insert the work between the centers and screw up the tail center just snug enough to prevent the lathe dog from chattering when machine is in operation, Fig. 10-19.

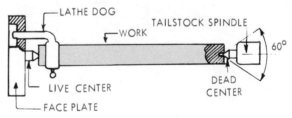

Fig. 10-19. Work mounted between centers.

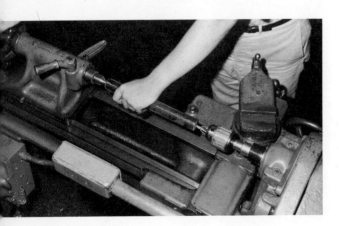

Fig. 10-17. Center drilling on the lathe.

13. Choose the proper lathe tool cutter bit for the job, Fig. 10-20.

14. Insert the tool holder in the tool post. Insert the cutter bit in the tool holder and tighten. Adjust

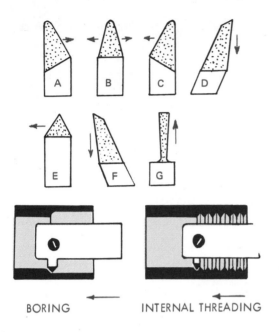

Fig. 10-20. Common lathe cutting tools. (A) Left-hand turning tool; (B) Round-nose turning tool; (C) Right-hand turning tool; (D) Left-hand facing tool; (E) Threading tool; (F) Right-hand facing tool; (G) Parting or cut-off tool.

Dia. in Inches	Cast Iron 75 f.p.m.	Machine Steel 100 f.p.m.	Soft Brass 200 f.p.m.	Aluminum 300 f.p.m.
1	287	382	764	1146
2	143	191	382	573
3	95	127	254	381
4	72	95	190	285
5	57	76	152	228
6	48	64	128	192
7	41	55	110	165
8	36	48	96	144
9	32	42	84	126
10	29	38	76	114

Fig. 10-22. Spindle speeds in revolutions per minute for average cuts with high-speed steel cutter bits.

the cutter bit and tool holder so the cutting edge of the tool is at the height of the lathe centers or a little above as shown in Fig. 10-21.

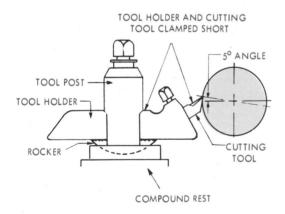

Fig. 10-21. Tool holder and cutting tool properly adjusted.

15. Adjust the lathe for the proper speed and feed. The cutting speed varies for different metals and for different sizes of stock. Feed is the distance the carriage, carrying the cutting tool, travels along the bed with each revolution of the spindle. Fig. 10-22 gives the cutting speed and feed for some of the more common metals.

16. The cut should be from the tailstock toward the headstock so the pressure is on the live center which turns with the work. Start the lathe and screw the cutter bit into the stock to take a cut. Engage the power fed and make the cut.

17. Check to see if the live and dead centers are in alignment as follows: After a complete cut has been made on the diameter and length of the stock, measure both ends with a micrometer. If the measurement is the same at both ends the centers are aligned. If the measurements are different, adjust the tailstock set-over screws and take another cut. Repeat these operations until both ends measure the same.

18. Adjust an outside caliper to 1/32 in. over the finished size. Turn on the lathe and turn the cross-feed handle to move the cutter bit into the work for a roughing cut that will true up the stock. Make a trial cut about 1/4 inch wide.

19. Turn the power off and check the trial cut with the calipers. Two or more roughing cuts may have to be taken.

20. Turn on the power and cut a little past the halfway point on the length of the stock. Continue cutting until the stock has been cut to within 1/32 in. of finished diameter. Remove the lathe dog and place it on the other end of the stock. Place the stock in the lathe and cut the other end to within 1/32 in. of the finished size.

21. Place a finishing cutter bit in the tool holder and make a trial cut about 1/4 in. long. Do not change cross-feed setting. Mike the cut. If the diameter for example, is .004 in. oversize, turn the cross-feed micrometer collar .002 in. in and take another trial cut. Check the diameter again with the mike. If the diameter is correct, make the longitudinal cut a little past the center.

22. Do not change the cross-feed setting. Remove the lathe dog. Place a band of aluminum or copper about 1/2 in. wide around the other end of the stock to protect the finished surface from the lathe dog screw. Slip the lathe dog over the soft metal band and clamp it in place.

23. Cut the other half of the stock to the finished size. When turning work to two or more diameters, cut the largest diameter first. Mark the stock at the first shoulder and cut this diameter. Continue this procedure until the smallest diameter has been turned.

A very smooth, brightly polished finish can be obtained by using fine grades of abrasive cloth after filing. Apply oil on the emery cloth and adjust the lathe to run at high speed. Keep the abrasive cloth moving slowly from one end to the other.

SAMMY SAFETY
SAYS:

"Keep your sleeves rolled up and hold your left elbow high so it will not be hit by the revolving lathe dog. Be careful not to let the emery cloth wrap around the revolving work."

TURNING A TAPER

Short tapers, such as those on a lathe center or center punch can be turned by clamping stock in a lathe chuck and setting the compound rest to the desired degree of taper. The point of the cutter bit is set on center and the carriage is locked in place. Make the cut by turning the compound rest feed screw, Fig. 10-25. Cut length is limited to compound rest travel.

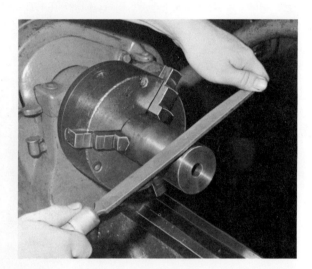

Fig. 10-23. Filing in the lathe. Keep the left arm well above the revolving chuck.

FILING AND POLISHING

Tool marks can be removed and a smooth, bright finish can be obtained on the surface of a piece by filing and polishing, Fig. 10-23. Use a fine mill file or a long-angle lathe file, Fig. 10-24. Adjust the lathe so

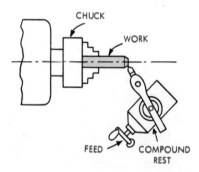

Fig. 10-25. Using the compound rest to cut a taper.

Fig. 10-24. A long-angle lathe file.   (Nicholson File Co.)

that the work will make two or three revolutions for each stroke of the file. Take long, even strokes across the metal. File just enough to obtain a smooth surface. Always keep your file clean and free from chips with a file card.

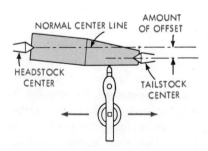

Fig. 10-26. Tailstock off-set to cut a taper.

Long tapers are turned by off-setting the tailstock, Fig. 10-26, or by means of a taper attachment. To find the amount of tailstock set-over for a taper, use this formula:

$$\text{Set-over} = \frac{\text{total length}}{\text{length to be tapered}} \times$$

$$\frac{\text{large diameter minus small diameter}}{2}$$

When the taper per foot is known use this formula:

$$\text{Set-over} = \frac{\text{taper per foot, in inches}}{2} \times$$

$$\frac{\text{length of piece}}{12}$$

LATHE CHUCKS

Lathe chucks are used to hold work that cannot be mounted between lathe centers. There are many machining operations which can be performed on work held in a chuck, such as turning, threading (internal and external), boring (straight and taper), reaming, and cutting off stock.

There are several types of chucks used for machining, the most popular being the 4-jaw independent chuck and the 3-jaw universal chuck, Fig. 10-27.

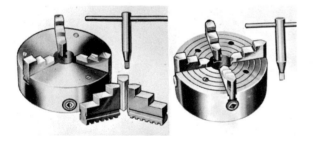

Fig. 10-27. Lathe chucks. Left, 3-jaw universal chuck. Right, 4-jaw independent chuck.   (South Bend Lathe)

The 4-jaw independent has four reversible jaws which can be independently adjusted. It will hold round, square and irregular shapes. The work can be adjusted to practically any degree of accuracy required. The 3-jaw universal chuck will hold round and hexagonal stock. The jaws move in or out together and automatically center the work within about three thousandths of an inch. This chuck is usually provided with one set of jaws for outside chucking, and

another set for inside chucking. The jaws cannot be reversed. The 3-jaw universal chuck is not used where extreme accuracy is required.

USING LATHE CHUCKS

When mounting a chuck on the lathe spindle, thoroughly clean and oil the threads of the spindle and the chuck back. A very small chip or burr will prevent the chuck from running smoothly. Remove the live center by holding the center with your right hand and giving the center a sharp tap with the knock out bar through the spindle hole. Place a piece of wood across the ways of the lathe to protect them. Grip the chuck by placing your fingers in the center between the jaws, and lift it onto the piece of wood. Turn the headstock spindle with the left hand and guide the chuck onto the thread. Be sure to get the chuck started squarely on the threads. The chuck should screw on easily. Continue to screw the chuck onto the spindle by hand until it is tight against the shoulder. Never bring the chuck against the spindle shoulder with a bang since this will make it difficult to remove.

To remove a chuck from the lathe spindle, engage the back gears and place a wood block between a chuck jaw and the back ways of the bed. Turn the spindle pulley by hand to loosen the chuck. Then place a board across the ways under the chuck. Continue to screw the chuck off by hand.

To mount the work in a 4-jaw independent chuck, open the four jaws an equal distance from the center. Use the concentric rings on the face of the chuck as a guide. Insert the work and tighten the jaws until it is approximately centered and held firmly. The work is then centered more accurately by bringing a piece of chalk in contact with the work as the chuck is slowly rotated, Fig. 10-28. The jaw opposite the chalk mark

Fig. 10-28. Centering work by the chalk method.

is loosened slightly. Then tighten the jaw on the side where the chalk mark is located. Continue this procedure until the work is centered. Check all four jaws to be sure they are securely tightened before starting to machine the work.

To mount work in a 3-jaw universal chuck, open jaws until the work can be inserted. Then tighten jaws with chuck key. Be sure to remove the key.

FACING

The term facing refers to the cutting or squaring of the end of a piece of work, as in Fig. 10-29. The

Fig. 10-30. Drilling in the lathe with a taper-shank drill. The drill is held in a drill chuck if it is a straight-shank.

Fig. 10-29. Facing in the lathe.

Fig. 10-31. Hand reaming in the lathe. Do not use power when hand reaming.

cutting tool is set so the cutting edge passes through the center of the work. Roughing cuts are made from the outside of the work toward the center. Finishing cuts are made from the center to the outside. Lock the carriage in place when making facing cuts.

DRILLING

Drilling on the lathe is done by holding the work in the lathe chuck and securing the drill in the tailstock, Fig. 10-30. After the work has been faced, spot the center for the drill with the cutter bit. Adjust the lathe to the correct speed for drilling. Select a drill 1/64 in. undersize to allow for reaming. Insert the drill in the tailstock. Drills with straight shanks are chucked in a drill chuck that has a tapered shank which will fit the taper in the tailstock. Bring the tailstock close to the work, so the tailstock spindle will not have to be run out any farther than

necessary to drill the hole. After the hole has been drilled, hand ream it in the lathe, Fig. 10-31. If a large hole is to be drilled, it is good practice to drill a pilot hole first.

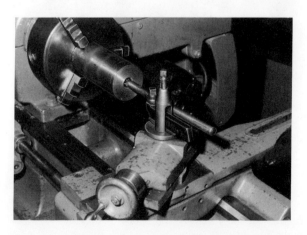

Fig. 10-32. Boring in the lathe with a boring bar.

BORING

Boring is done when the hole to be cut is not standard size, or to cut a very accurate hole. Use a boring tool holder with a bar which can be adjusted, so the cutting edge of the tool is in the proper position for cutting, Fig. 10-32.

THREADING

A lathe may be used to cut a great variety of threads. This is done by using a specially sharpened tool bit. The power feed is adjusted to move the carriage along at a rate that will cause the tool to cut the required number of threads per inch. This is a very fascinating operation. Ask your teacher for a demonstration.

An easy method for cutting internal threads, although not as accurate, is to use a tap in a lathe. Place the center hole of the tap on the point of the dead center and the work end of the tap in the (tap) drilled hole of the work, Fig. 10-33. Adjust the

Fig. 10-33. Tapping in the lathe.

tailstock so there is just enough pressure to hold the tap in place. Turn the tap with a cresent wrench. After each turn of the tap it will be necessary to readjust the tailstock center. It is not necessary to complete the job in the lathe. After the threads have been started straight with the taper tap, the threading can be completed at the bench with the plug and bottoming tap.

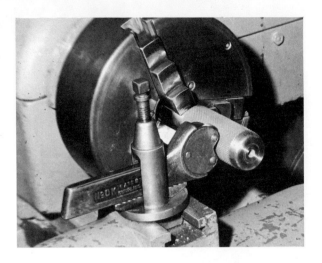

Fig. 10-34. Using lathe for knurling.

KNURLING

Knurling is a process of embossing the surface of the work, Fig. 10-34. Some pieces of work and handles of tools are knurled to provide a better gripping surface. Knurling tools are available which will produce fine, medium, coarse, straight, and diamond patterns.

The knurling tool is clamped in the tool post at right angles to the work. Adjust the lathe for the slowest back geared speed. Mark off the space to be knurled. Start the lathe and force the knurling tool into the work at the right end. The knurls should be pressed hard into the work at the start and then the pressure is relieved a little after making sure they track. Use plenty of oil to lubricate the knurling wheels regardless of the kind of material being knurled. Then engage the longitudinal feed of the carriage and let the knurling tool feed across the work to the left. To make a deeper cut reverse the lathe spindle and let the knurling tool feed back to the starting point. Do not remove the knurl from the impression. Force the tool deeper into the work, and let it feed back across the work. Repeat this procedure until the knurling is finished.

THE SHAPER

The shaper is a machine tool which has the cutting tool mounted in a ram, Fig. 10-35. The ram moves back and forth horizontally across the work. This machine can be used for shaping horizontal, vertical,

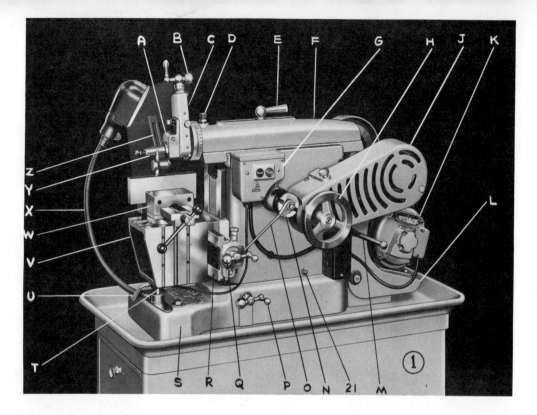

Fig. 10-35. Principal parts of a shaper: (A) Clapper box, (B) Down-feed handle, (C) Head, (D) Headswivel lock screw, (E) Ram clamping handle, (F) Ram, (G) Switch box, (H) Hand wheel, (J) Drive-pulley guard, (K) Motor, (L) Motor cradle, (M) Tension release lever, (N) Eccentric, (O) Feed rod, (P) Table elevating crank, (Q) Cross feed crank, (R) Cross-rail, (S) Base, (T) Work-table support, (U) Support locking handle, (V) Work-table, (W) Vise, (X) Lamp, (Y) Tool post, (Z) Tool holder.   (South Bend Lathe)

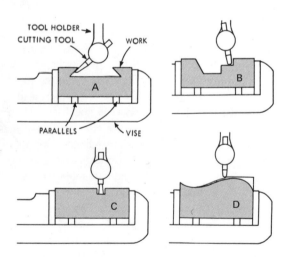

Fig. 10-36. Cuts that can be made on a shaper: (A) Angular cuts; (B) Horizontal; Vertical, and Angular cuts; (C) Slotting cut; (D) Simple form cutting.

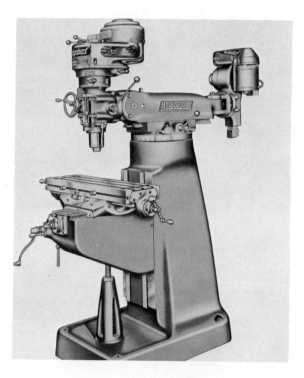

Fig. 10-37. Vertical milling machine. (Bridgeport Machines, Inc.)

angular and curved surfaces, Fig. 10-36. The work is either mounted in the vise, or clamped to the table. The table can be moved vertically or horizontally. The shaper size is determined by the maximum stroke in inches, such as 7 in., 12 in., 16 in., and 24 in. Except for some of the tool angles, the shaper

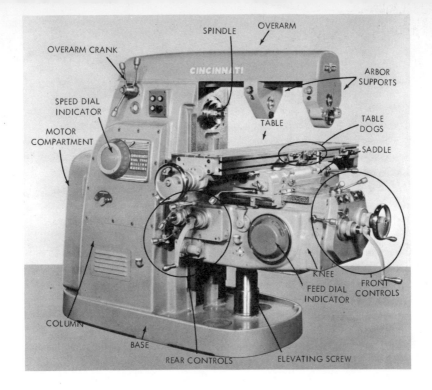

Fig. 10-38. Horizontal milling machine. (Cincinnati Milling Machine Co.)

cutting tools are the same as those used in the lathe. Since the shaper cuts on the forward stroke only, the side-relief angle needs to be only about 3 or 4 degrees. The end-relief angle, or front clearance, should be approximately 3 or 4 degrees.

THE MILLING MACHINE

The milling machine produces one or more machined surfaces on the work. The work is clamped to the table of the machine, or held in a fixture or jig which is clamped to the table. A rotating cutter shapes and smoothes the metal. There are several types of milling machines. The two most commonly found in the school shop are the Vertical Milling Machine, Fig. 10-37, and the Plain Horizontal Milling Machine, Fig. 10-38. These machines are known as knee-and-column type because the spindle is fixed in the column. The table (which is a part of the knee) can be adjusted longitudinally, transversely and vertically. Milling machines can be used to cut straight or irregular surfaces, slots, and grooves. They can also be used to cut gear teeth. Some milling operations are shown in Fig. 10-39 and Fig. 10-40.

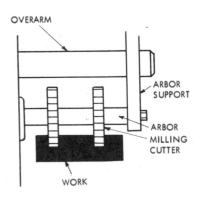

Fig. 10-40. Gang milling---cutting two slots in a block of metal.

NEW METAL FORMING TECHNIQUES

The development of super-tough alloys and the requirements of the space-age production line has brought about many new techniques for doing special

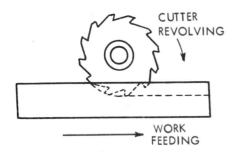

Fig. 10-39. Milling a slot in a block of metal.

jobs. Several of these new methods are described in the paragraphs that follow. You will probably want to study these techniques in more depth if you are planning to pursue a career in the metalworking field.

EXPLOSIVE FORMING

This is a technique used to shape sheet metal. Although it was first used to shape small parts, today this method is used to make aerospace components. Existing presses are either too small or they do not have the power needed to fabricate the high-strength space-age metals. Another advantage of explosive forming is that no welded joints are required. This process makes use of a pressure wave which is generated by an explosion in a fluid. The pressure wave forces the walls of the metal being shaped against the walls of the die.

ELECTROCHEMICAL MILLING

This process shapes metal by removing part of the metal by deep etching. The amount of metal removed can be controlled and held to close tolerances. The technique makes it possible to shape metal parts that would be most difficult to do using conventional machining methods. Parts are immersed in an etching solution. A maskant (resistant material) is used to cover any surface not to be machined. The amount of metal removed is controlled by the length of time it is immersed.

ELECTRICAL DISCHARGE MACHINING

This is the process of removing metal by high current, low-voltage electrical spark (arcing) discharge which takes place between the tool and the metal being machined. The electrode, which is the shape to be cut, and the workpiece are submerged in a dielectric fluid during the machining process. This technique has the following advantages: metals that have been heat-treated can be machined. Also, fragile, hard, tough, heat sensitive metals that would be difficult to machine by conventional methods can be worked to close tolerances.

LASER MACHINING

This process is used in machining, cutting, and welding operations. A narrow and intense beam of light is produced by the laser. This beam of light can be focused optically into an area which is a few microns (thousandths of a millimeter) in diameter. Temperatures up to 75,000 deg. F can be created instantaneously at the point of focus. Because of this intense heat, the beam of light can penetrate any material known to man. Use of the laser is being researched not only in metalworking but in many other areas including the field of medicine.

OTHER TECHNIQUES

There are several other techniques which you may want to research and write reports for additional credit. These include magnetic forming, ultrasonic machining, electron beam machining, spark forming, and gas forming. You will find these techniques provide some interesting, unique methods which industry is using to form metal.

QUIZ — UNIT 10

1. The tool and diemaker must have a knowledge about _____, _____ and _____.
2. An outside caliper is used to take _____, _____.
3. An inside caliper is used to take _____.
4. If the reading on the micrometer sleeve is two divisions past the one and the thimble reading is 15, the reading would be _____.
5. What is a metal lathe?
6. A combination drill and countersink is used to _____ for _____ turning.
7. For very accurate turning you should use the _____ chuck.
8. Name two ways to turn tapers in a lathe.
9. List five operations that can be performed in a lathe.
10. Describe the use of a shaper.
11. What is the difference between a vertical mill and a horizontal mill?

METALWORKING PROJECTS

The projects covered in this Unit are examples of what can be constructed to assist you in your study of the various units of metal work. Your instructor may also have other projects which you will want to consider. You can also get ideas for additional projects by visiting gift shops and department stores and from magazines and catalogues.

The projects illustrated in this Unit have been selected to provide easy ones for the beginning metalworking student to construct. Others which are more difficult to make have also been included to present a challenge to the student and to give him experience in problem solving as he develops more proficiency in the metals area. These projects lend themselves to many different designs and construction methods. You may want to change the size of some of these plans to fit your own needs. For example, the shelf may be too large, or you might want to hang your house number sign on a post which will require a different bracket.

HOUSE NUMBER SIGN

This house number sign, Fig. 11-1, is a good beginning project. Its construction involves some important hand tool operations which can be applied to numerous other projects. You may want to change the design of the scroll work or the shape of the plate which holds the numbers. Patterns for the numbers can be made so they can be cast in the foundry or they may be cut from aluminum or brass sheet stock.

MATERIAL:

Standard: 1 pc. band iron 1/8 x 1/2 x 37 in.
Scrolls: 1 pc. band iron 1/8 x 1/2 x 21 in.
Plate: 1 pc. black iron 22 ga. 5 x 14 in.
Hooks: 1 pc. mild steel 1/8 in. dia. x 7 in.
Rivets: 4 black iron 1/8 x 1/2 in. round head.
Numbers: Aluminum or brass — cast in foundry, cut from sheet stock, or purchase.

Fig. 11-1. House number sign.

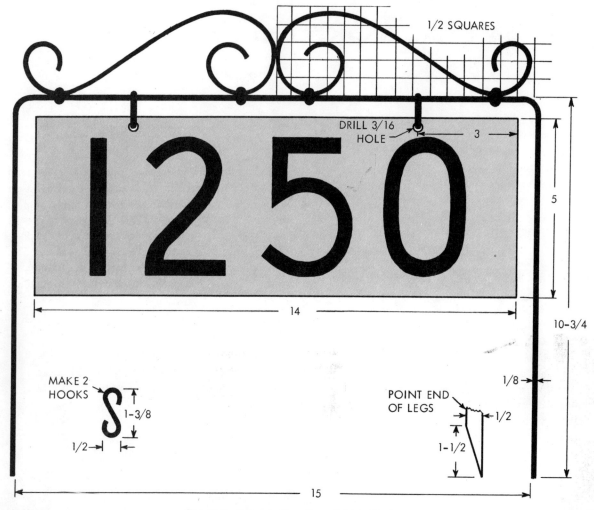

Fig. 11-2. House number sign, working drawing.

PROCEDURE:

1. Draw a full-size pattern of the scroll on squared paper. See Fig. 11-2.
2. Figure the amount of material needed for the scrolls and cut to correct length.
3. Square the ends of the metal and remove burrs.
4. Form the scrolls.
5. Cut material to length for the standard.
6. Lay out pointed ends on both legs of the standard.
7. Cut the ends to shape and file the edges.
8. Mark off bends on material for standard.
9. Make 90-deg. bends with a small radius as shown on drawing.
10. Lay out number plate on 22 ga. black iron.
11. Cut number plate to size, and file all edges.
12. Lay out location of holes.
13. Center punch and drill holes.

14. Cut out stock for hooks.
15. Form hooks.
16. Locate rivet holes on scrolls and center punch.
17. Drill 1/8 in. dia. holes in scrolls.
18. Locate rivet holes on the standard and center punch.
19. Drill 1/8 in. dia. holes in the standard.
20. Rivet the scrolls to the standard.
21. Draw full-size pattern of figures on metal. (If you cast your figures in the foundry, skip procedure 21 and 22).
22. Cut out figures and polish.
23. Locate rivet holes on figures.
24. Center punch and drill holes in figures for rivets.
25. Rivet figures to both sides of the plate.
26. Paint as desired.
27. Insert hooks in the standard and attach the number plate.

WALL PLANT HOLDER

This wall plant holder, Fig. 11-3, is an attractive planter for displaying trailing vines and green plants. Flattened expanded metal or perforated metal can be used for the back, Fig. 11-4. All pieces are joined with

Fig. 11-3. Wall plant holder.

solder. While soft solder, properly applied will serve satisfactorily, hard soldering will make the project stronger. If you have a spot welder in your shop, the expanded metal can be joined to the wire frame with it very easily. All of the metal parts must be cleaned thoroughly before applying the finish. This project is very attractive when given a satin black finish.

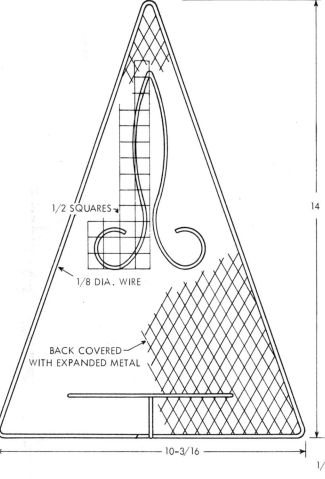

1/2 SQUARES

14

1/8 DIA. WIRE

BACK COVERED WITH EXPANDED METAL

10-3/16

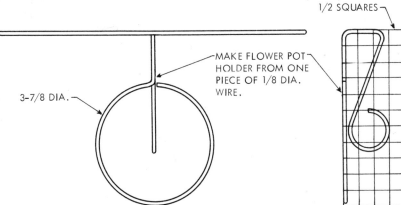

1/2 SQUARES

MAKE FLOWER POT HOLDER FROM ONE PIECE OF 1/8 DIA. WIRE.

3-7/8 DIA.

Fig. 11-4. Wall plant holder, working drawing.

PICTURE EASEL

A picture easel is a project that can be used to add a decorative touch to any room. The easel may be constructed of band iron or strips of 16 gage brass. Follow pattern, Fig. 11-6. The trough that holds the picture can be made from 22 gage sheet iron or 20 gage sheet brass. Note that a chain is used to keep the easel tripod leg from opening too far. The metal strips can be decorated by peening. All parts should be fastened together by soldering (hard solder preferred). A unique and attractive finish can be obtained on band iron by painting the project flat black, then highlighting all of the parts with gold Rub'N Buff. If you use brass to construct your project, it is suggested that you polish the brass pieces and finish with metal lacquer, Fig. 11-5.

Fig. 11-5. Picture easel.

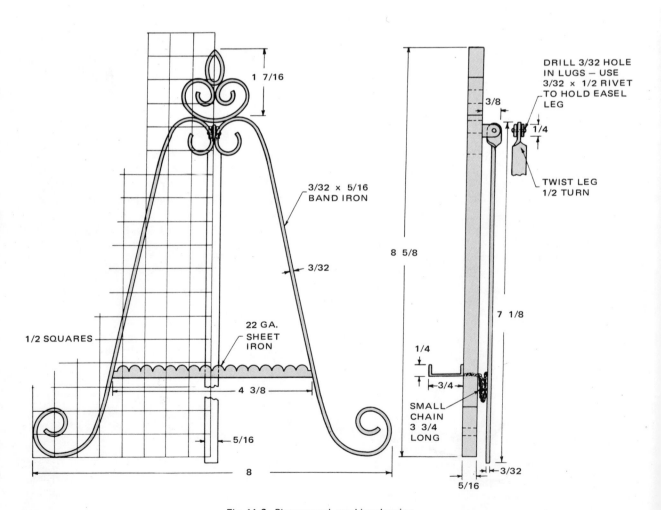

Fig. 11-6. Picture easel, working drawing.

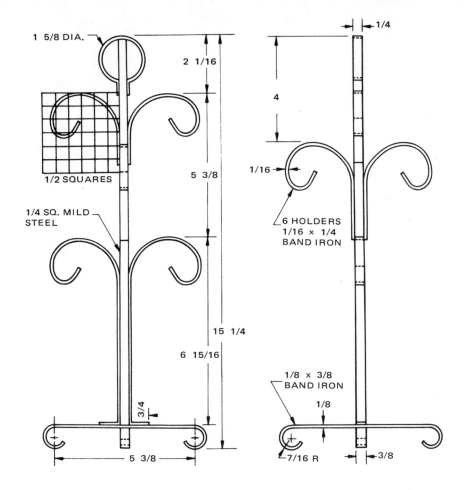

Fig. 11-7. Mug holder, working drawing.

MUG HOLDER

This project provides an attractive way to hang up your coffee, tea, or hot chocolate mug. The first step of procedure is to make a full size drawing of the cup hangers by enlarging the squares as indicated on the working drawing, Fig. 11-7. You will notice that the four cup hangers located at the upper portion of the stand have a stem 1 3/8 inches long which is fastened to the stand. The two lower hangers require a stem 6 inches long. A 3/4 in. section is bent 90 degrees to the base--this portion provides support for the stand. After all of the pieces have been cut to size and properly formed, you are ready for assembly. The parts of your mug holder may be spot welded together or you might choose to use rivets for this operation. After the holder has been assembled, you will need to adjust the base so all four ends of the scroll touch the surface of your work bench and do not allow the holder to rock. The finish can be a bright enamel color which will match the decor of the room where the holder will be used. See Fig. 11-8.

Fig. 11-8. Mug holder.

WROUGHT IRON TABLE

Here is a project that you will find interesting to construct and a very useful piece of furniture. Construction is simple and it provides you with an opportunity to do some welding. It will be necessary for you to draw a full-size pattern, Fig. 11-10, of the leg by enlarging the squares to one inch. After you have formed the legs to the shape of your pattern, form the 14 in. dia. and the 4 in. dia. rings. The top end of the legs provide a support for the plastic disc top. Weld the legs to the top ring 3/16 in. from the top. This will allow the 3/16 in. plastic disc to rest on the legs and be flush with the top edge of the ring. You may want to design a jig to hold the legs in place while welding them to the two rings. The feet can be made out of brass or you might choose to use rubber tips that are commonly used on wrought iron furniture. The finish for this project should include a metal primer for the undercoat and metal enamel of the desired color for the finish coat. See Fig. 11-9.

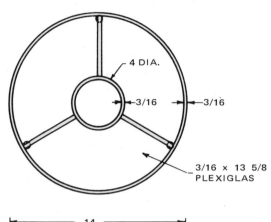

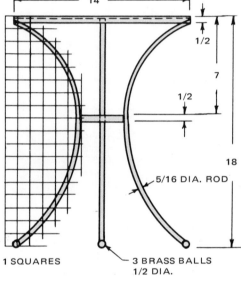

Fig. 11-10. Wrought iron table, working drawing.

Fig. 11-9. Wrought iron table.

OWL TRIVET

This is a handy project that will keep the hot dishes from damaging the finish on a table or counter top. You will want to select a piece of heavy gage sheet metal such as .080 in. thick aluminum or 12 gage brass. Make a full-size pattern on a piece of tracing paper and glue it to the piece of metal selected with rubber cement. Drill 1/8 in. holes in each of the areas to be cut out. A jeweler's saw or a scroll saw equipped with a metal cutting blade may be used to cut out the owl. Attach cork discs to the bottom of the owl as indicated on the drawing, Fig. 11-12. Also, see Fig. 11-11.

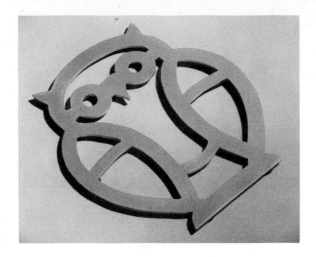

Fig. 11-11. Owl trivet.

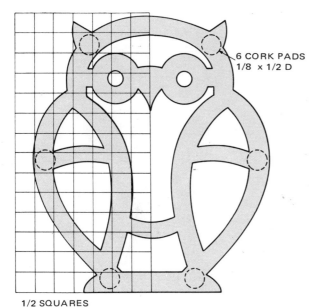

6 CORK PADS
1/8 x 1/2 D

1/2 SQUARES

Fig. 11-12. Owl trivet, working drawing.

METAL SWTICH PLATE

This attractive plate protects the wall finish and helps keep the wall clean around an electric switch. You may want to draw your own design. The dimensions given for the screw holes and the cut outs for the switch lever are standard and will fit all junction boxes. A single switch plate can be made using these dimensions. Remember that only two screw holes and one switch lever slot will be needed. The drawing, Fig. 11-14, indicates that the plate is raised 3/16 in. at the center. This allows the plate to

fit flush against the wall. You will note that the screw holes are formed (countersunk) to receive screws with oval heads. The surface of the plate may be decorated with different shaped peen marks. 24 oz. copper or 20 ga. brass makes a very attractive plate. Finish the plate with metal lacquer. See Fig. 11-13.

Fig. 11-13. Metal switch plate.

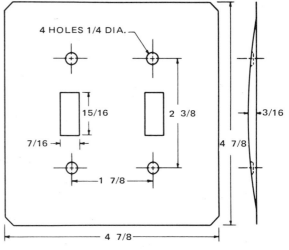

4 HOLES 1/4 DIA.

15/16

2 3/8

7/16

1 7/8

3/16

4 7/8

4 7/8

Fig. 11-14. Metal switch plate, working drawing.

Fig. 11-15. Beverage glass holder.

BEVERAGE GLASS HOLDER

This project comes in handy at the drive-in or when you are traveling. The holder is made out of .032 in. half-hard sheet aluminum. The ends of the band lap over each other on the rear side of the back piece that hooks onto the car window glass, Fig. 11-15. Two rivets, as indicated in the drawing, Fig. 11-16, provide a good method for fastening the band to the back piece. A satin finish is recommended. You·may want to change the dimensions given in the drawing to fit beverage glasses which are larger or smaller.

Fig. 11-17. Magazine rack.

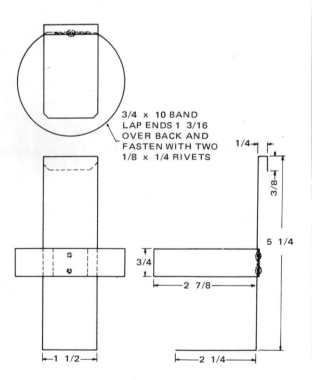

3/4 x 10 BAND LAP ENDS 1 3/16 OVER BACK AND FASTEN WITH TWO 1/8 x 1/4 RIVETS

Fig. 11-16. Beverage glass holder, working drawing.

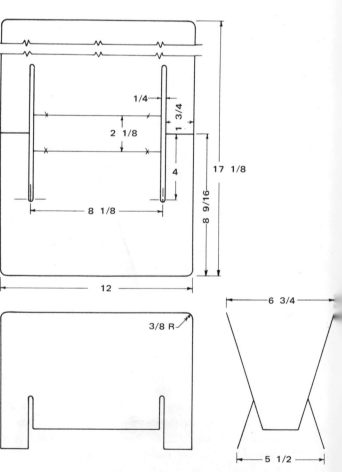

Fig. 11-18. Magazine rack, working drawing.

RACK FOR MAGAZINES

This is a unique project made from one piece of sheet metal. One-half hard aluminum .064 in. thick works real well, although sheet iron is less expensive and works satisfactorily. Lay out the pattern on the selected metal sheet and cut the stock to size as indicated in the drawing, Fig. 11-18. Drill the ends of the two slots with a 1/4 in. drill. Cut the part which forms the legs and finish cutting out the slots. All of the corners should be rounded with a file. Carefully bend the metal to form the rack as shown on the drawing. Select a finish that fits the decor of the room where you will use the rack. See Fig. 11-17.

CHISEL AND PUNCH SET

A set of chisels and punches added to your tool kit will come in handy for many jobs. Use square tool steel to make these tools. The punches are turned to shape on a lathe. The chisels are forged to shape. Using these designs you can make various sizes of chisels and punches for your set. Round off the striking end in a lathe as indicated in the drawing, Fig. 11-20. After you have shaped your chisels and punches they are ready to be heat treated. It is

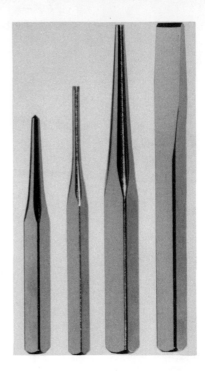

Fig. 11-19. Chisel and punch set.

suggested that you polish the rounded ends and the work end of these tools. The center punch point and the cutting edge of the chisel are ground to the proper shape on a tool grinder. See Fig. 11-19.

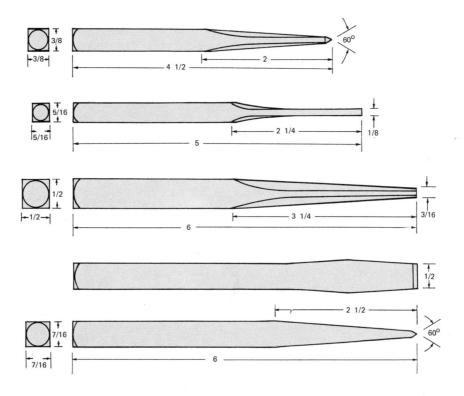

Fig. 11-20. Chisel and punch set, working drawing.

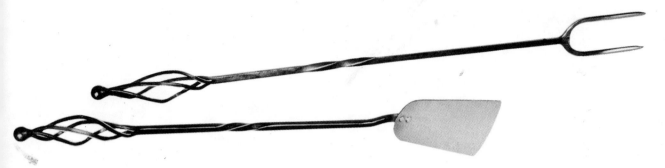

Fig. 11-21. Barbecue tools.

BARBECUE TOOLS

The barbecue tools shown in Fig. 11-21 have very unique spiral handles which are sure to make them conversation pieces. They look difficult to make but the spiral handle is really very simple to form. Slot one end of the handle as shown in Fig. 11-22. Braze or weld the ends of the four prongs together. If you do not have equipment to braze or weld the pieces, the slots can be made by drilling 1/16 inch holes along the slots until you can insert a hacksaw blade to finish the cuts. Start drilling the holes 1/4 in. from the end of the handle. The spirals are formed by clamping the end of the metal in a vise and twisting the metal with a wrench. The jaws of the wrench should grip the metal close to the end of the slots. As

the metal is twisted it will become shorter and cause the four prongs to spread and twist. If the prongs do not spread evenly, shape them with a pair of pliers. The twist in the solid part of the handles is formed by clamping one end of the section to be twisted close to the edge of the vise jaws. Place the jaws of a wrench at the other end of the section and twist. The spatula and fork can be made of stainless steel, hard tempered aluminum, or sheet steel. The fork and spatula should be polished. The handles can be finished by coating them with oil and heating the metal until the oil is burned off. Then the surface of the metal should be polished, using a soft clean rag to produce a smooth satin sheen.

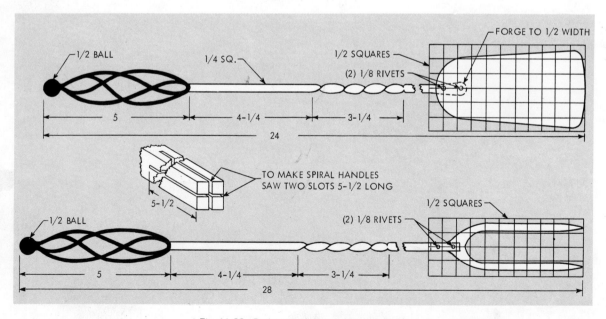

Fig. 11-22. Barbecue tools, working drawing.

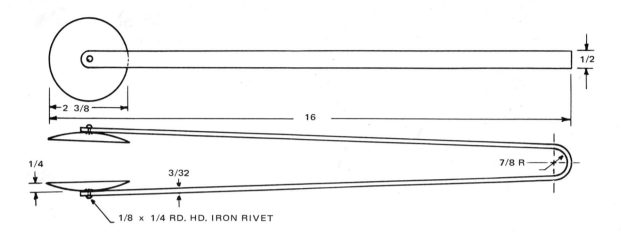

Fig. 11-23. Charcoal tongs.

CHARCOAL TONGS

These tongs are a must if you like to barbecue with charcoal. They are simple to construct, Fig. 11-23. Use cold rolled steel for the handle since this kind of metal has just the right amount of hardness to create the spring-back needed to open the discs when releasing the coals. The two discs can be made from 24 gage sheet iron. Hammer the discs to shape over a stake or a hard wood form that has been hollowed out. The discs can be riveted or spot welded to the handle. A heat resistant black paint is recommended to insure a satisfactory bond between the metal and the paint. See Fig. 11-24.

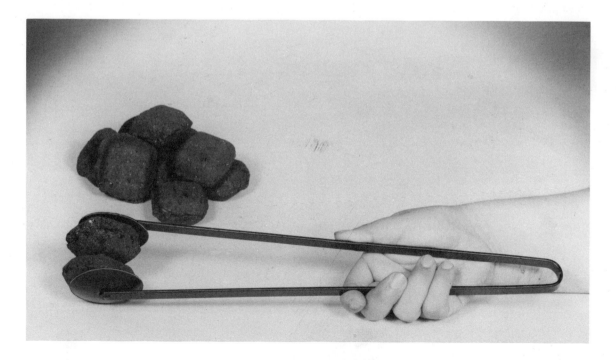

Fig. 11-24. Charcoal tongs, working drawing.

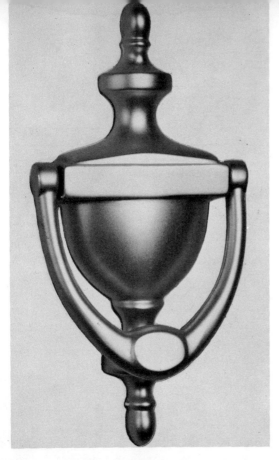

Fig. 11-25. Door knocker.

DOOR KNOCKER

The classic grace of Colonial design in the door knocker, Fig. 11-25, will add distinction to any door. It may be cast in aluminum or brass. The pattern can either be carved out of wood or modeled in clay which is used to make a plaster of Paris mold. The plaster of Paris mold is then used to cast a metal pattern that can be used for green sand foundry work. A hole is drilled in the back side of the knocker plate at the top and at the bottom for a 10-24 machine screw to attach the knocker to a door. The striker is fastened to the plate with two rivets, Fig. 11-26. If aluminum is used, a satin finish is very attractive. Brass is generally given a buffed finish, and should be lacquered to prevent tarnishing.

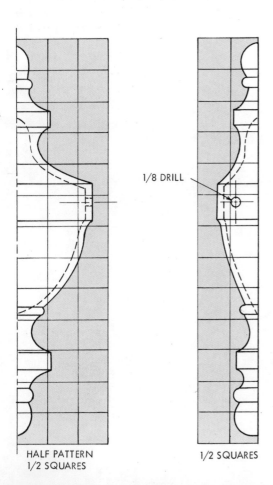

1/8 DRILL

HALF PATTERN
1/2 SQUARES

1/2 SQUARES

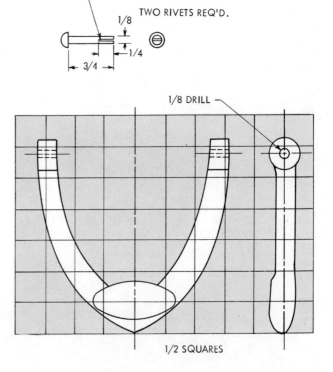

CUT SLOT WITH HACKSAW

TWO RIVETS REQ'D.

1/8

3/4

1/4

1/8 DRILL

1/2 SQUARES

Fig. 11-26. Door knocker, working drawing.

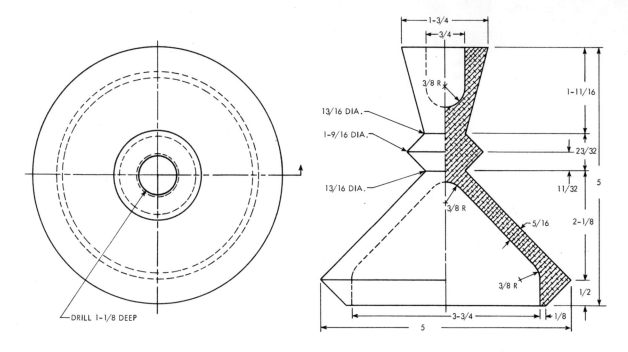

Fig. 11-27. Candle holder, working drawing.

CANDLE HOLDER

The light reflections given off of the flat tapered surfaces of the candle holder, Fig. 11-28, makes it a most beautiful piece that will blend with modern or traditional trends. This project requires two patterns and a core mold. A one-piece pattern is made for the base, and a split-pattern is used for the stem and holder. A shank is cast on each part to provide a means for chucking. The hole for the candle is formed with a core. The project is attractive cast in either aluminum or brass. Turn the holder to shape in the lathe and drill and tap the stem for a 10-24 x 1 in. machine screw. Turn the base to shape, and drill a clearance hole through the center for a 10-24 machine screw which is used to join the holder and stem to the base, Fig. 11-27. A highly buffed polish brings out the beauty in this project.

Fig. 11-28. Candle holder.

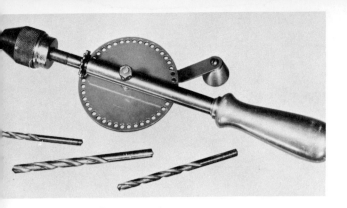

Fig. 11-29. Hand drill.

HAND DRILL

This hand drill is an interesting and challenging project. All of the parts can be made of mild steel except the handle which should be made of aluminum or wood to give the tool better balance. A 3-jaw, 1/4 in. chuck can be purchased. The chuck shaft gear and the drive wheel are the pieces which are most difficult to make. The drive wheel must be accurately laid out and drilled in order to work properly. The teeth on the gear are made by drilling 3/64 in. holes between them, close to the root circle, and then cutting out surplus metal left between the teeth with a hacksaw. Finish the gear by filing to the layout lines. A jig can be developed that can be used to drill evenly spaced holes in the drive wheel. See if you can design a jig for this operation. After all of the parts have been made, attach the drive wheel to the body of the drill. Insert the ball bearing and chuck shaft in the end of the body. Hold the chuck shaft tightly against the ball bearing, and adjust the gear on the shaft until the teeth match perfectly with the holes in the drive wheel. The chuck shaft gear can be attached by brazing. Or, you can use a 1/16 in. key between the shaft and the gear, and hard solder the pieces together. After gear has been joined to shaft, assemble the drill, and test it. File off high spots on teeth of the gear that do not mesh, Figs. 11-29 and 11-30.

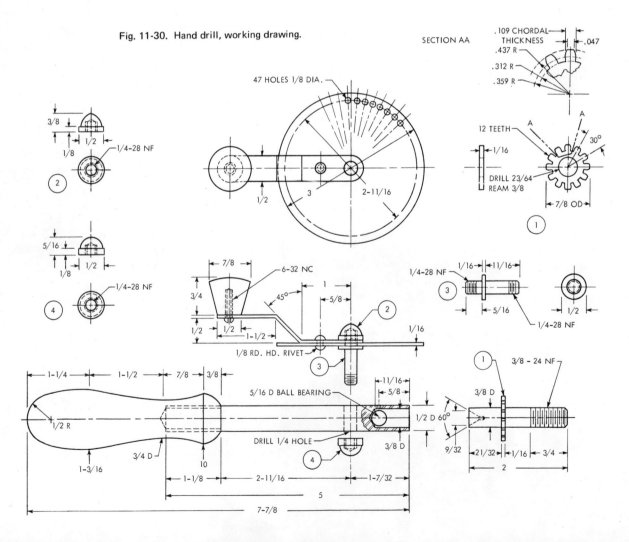

Fig. 11-30. Hand drill, working drawing.

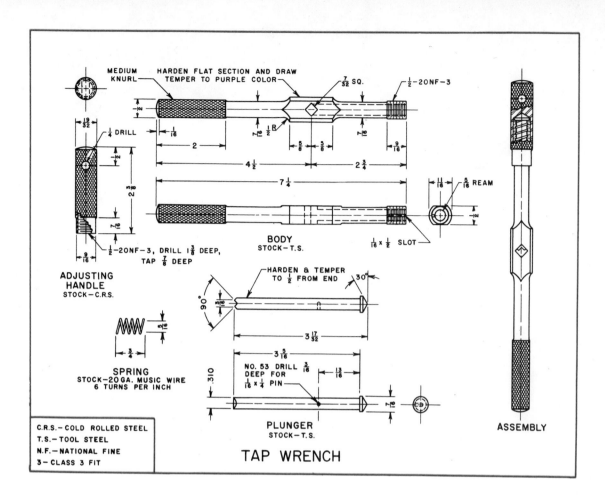

Fig. 11-31. Tap wrench, working drawing.

TAP WRENCH

The tap wrench, Fig. 11-32, is another tool that will come in handy and one that should be added to your tool kit. Follow the drawing, Fig. 11-31, to construct this project. All of the parts are made in the lathe, even the winding of the spring. The 9/16 in. hole in the end of the adjusting handle should be drilled and tapped in the lathe. The threads on the right end of the body can be threaded in the lathe, or with a threading die. If a threading die is used, great care must be taken to start the threads straight. The square hole in the body is made by drilling first with a 7/32 in. drill, then filing the hole square with a square file. The wrench parts which are made from cold rolled steel should be casehardened.

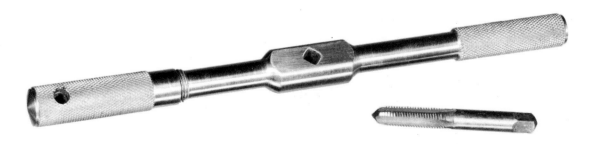

Fig. 11-32. Tap wrench.

109

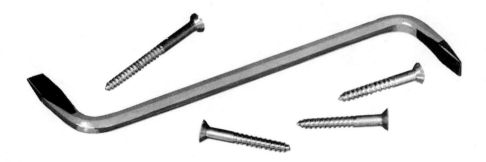

Fig. 11-33. Offset screwdriver.

OFFSET SCREWDRIVER

The offset screwdriver, Fig. 11-33, will come in handy for those hard-to-get-to places. You will want one in your tool kit. This tool is made of water hardened tool steel. Two or three different sizes of metal can be used to make a set. Forge the points of the blades to shape and anneal the metal. Then bend the offsets, harden and temper the points, as shown in Fig. 11-34.

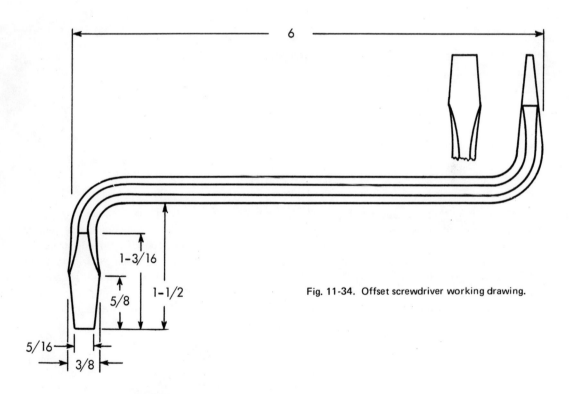

Fig. 11-34. Offset screwdriver working drawing.

BIRD FEEDER

The bird feeder, Fig. 11-35, will provide you with many interesting hours watching birds that visit the feeder. The house can be made of 24 ga. sheet metal. The front of the roof has a wired edge—use No. 16 wire, Fig. 11-36. The perch is made of 1/2 O.D. aluminum tubing. Fasten the perch to the floor of the feeder with either round-head machine screws, or rivets. The roof and the floor of the feeder can be joined to the sides by soldering, riveting, or spot welding. The pipe which can be used to attach the feeder to a pole is optional and depends on how you plan to hang your bird feeder. The finish should be a dark shade of green or brown since birds tend to be cautious of bright colors.

Fig. 11-35. Bird feeder.

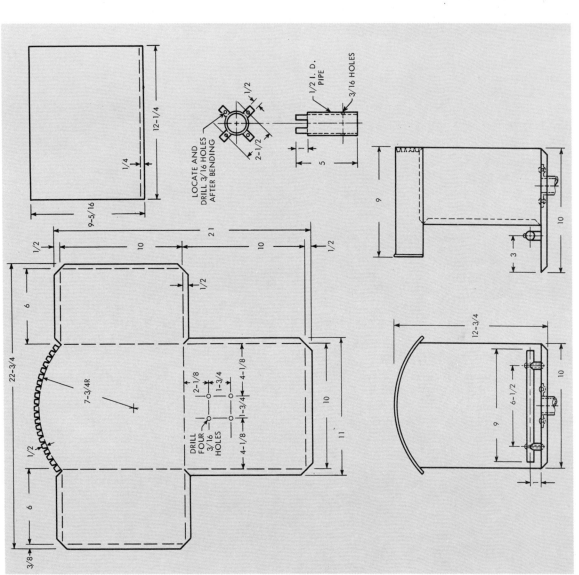

Fig. 11-36. Bird feeder, working drawing.

111

For these projects, only over-all dimensions and material suggestions have been included. Dimensions for individual parts have been omitted, so the development of the plans may be used to teach designing and problem solving.

METAL NAPKIN RACK

SIZE: 3 1/2 wide x 4 1/2 high x 5 1/4 long.
MATERIAL: Frame — 1/8 wire.
          Holder — 24 ga. perforated steel.
          Feet — 5/16 steel balls, or No. 13 1/8 dia. rubber tips.

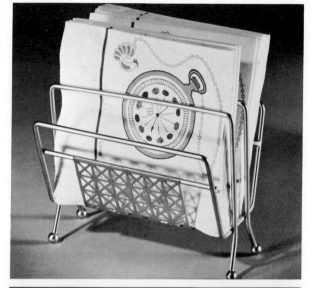

DISH WARMER — Uses Candle For Fuel

SIZE: 3 high x 5 1/4 wide x 6 long.
MATERIAL: Ends - wood or 24 oz. copper.
          Handles — 1/2 dia. maple dowel.
          Slides — 16 oz. copper.
          Grill — 1/8 square copper bars.
          Candle Holder — 20 ga. sheet iron.
          Candle Holder Support — 1/8 dia. wire.
          Rivets — 1/4 x 3/32 dia. copper or 1/2 No. 16 Round head Escutcheon Pins if wood ends are used.

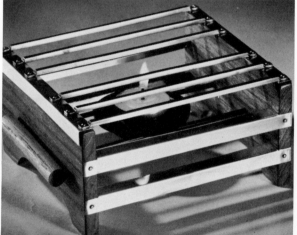

TOOLS FOR POTTED PLANT GARDENERS

SIZE: Holder — 2 1/2 x 3 x 6 1/8.
          Spade — 6 1/8 long, 1 5/8 wide.
          Rake — 4 5/8 long x 2 wide.
MATERIAL: Tool Holder —
          Base — 1/2 x 2 1/2 x 3 cast aluminum.
          Standard — 5/16 dia. steel rod.
          Standard Knob - 1/2 dia. steel rod.
          Plastic Flower — Small.
          Tool Holder — 3/32 dia. wire.
          Spade —
          Handle — 1/4 dia. brass rod.
          Blade — .040 thick sheet brass.
          Rake —
          Handle — 1/4 dia. brass rod.
          Teeth — .064 thick sheet brass.

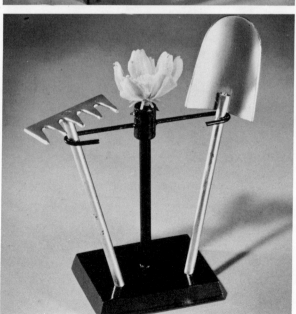

HARDWARE SCULPTURE

The hardware sculptures are fun to create. They are constructed from springs, nuts, bolts, wing nuts, nails, tubing, sheet metal, etc. — pieces from the metal scrap box. Keep sizes of materials in proper proportion.

MAILBOX

SIZE: 5 deep x 6 high x 14 3/4 long.
MATERIAL: Body — 22 ga. sheet metal
            Lid and hinge — 20 ga. sheet metal.
            Magazine holder — 26 ga. spring steel.
            Hinge pin — 3/32 wire.

WALL SCULPTURE

SIZE: Approximately 22 in. x 22 in.
MATERIAL: Old fashion iron nails 3 1/2 in. long.
NOTE: Weld the nails together to create the design. Other kinds of metal rods and strips of sheet metal can be used to form interesting sculptures.

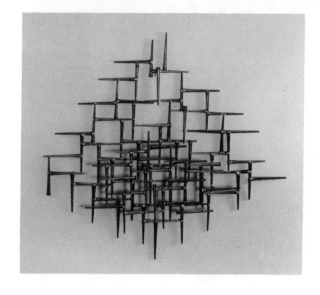

CANDLE HOLDERS

Wrought Iron Candle Holder
SIZE: 2 3/8 in. dia. base by 2 in. high.
MATERIAL: Base and stem — 1/4 in. sq. x 9 in. long mild steel. Candle holder disc — 18 ga. x 2 in. dia. sheet steel.

Pin (center of disc) — 1/16 in. dia. x 1/2 in. long.
NOTE: Twist the square rod and bend to form base and stem. Cut out 2 in. disc and cup it to form a dish 3/16 in. deep. File pin to a sharp point so it can be stuck into the center of the candle easily. Braze or hard solder the pin and disc to the top of the stem.

Leaf Candle Holder
SIZE: 3 1/4 in. wide x 4 3/4 in. long.
MATERIAL: Handle and base — 18 ga. sheet steel 1 1/8 in. wide x 5 3/4 in. long.

Leaf — 28 ga. sheet steel 3 1/4 in. wide x 3 3/8 in. long.

Pin — 1/8 in. dia. x 3/4 in. long mild steel.
NOTE: Make a maple leaf pattern and transfer to sheet steel. Cut out leaf and cup it to a dish shape. Cut out metal for handle and base (taper piece from 1 1/8 in. wide at one end to 5/16 in. wide at the other end) and bend it to form the base and handle. Taper the candle holder pin to a sharp point at one end. Drill a 1/8 in. hole through the center of the leaf. Press the pin into the hole in the leaf. Position the leaf on the base and solder the leaf to the base. Finish with semi-gloss black enamel.

FOR FURTHER STUDY

Althouse, A. D., Turnquist, C. H., and Bowditch, W. A., MODERN WELDING, The Goodheart-Willcox Co., South Holland, Illinois.

Feirer, John L., GENERAL METALS, McGraw-Hill Co., New York, New York.

Feirer, John L. and Lindbeck, John R., METALWORK, Chas. A. Bennett Co., Peoria, Illinois.

Fifer, Bill, METAL PROJECTS BOOK 2, The Goodheart-Willcox Co., South Holland, Illinois.

Glazner, Everett R., BASIC METALWORK TECHNOLOGY, Steck-Vaughn Co., Austin, Texas.

Johnson, Harold V., TECHNICAL METALS, Chas. A. Bennett Co., Peoria, Illinois.

Ludwig, O. A., and McCarthy, W. J., METALWORK TECHNOLOGY AND PRACTICE, McKnight Publishing Co., Bloomington, Illinois.

Smith, R. E., FORGING AND WELDING, McKnight Publishing Co., Bloomington, Illinois.

Smith, R. E., PATTERNMAKING AND FOUNDING, McKnight Publishing Co., Bloomington, Illinois.

Walker, John R., ARC WELDING, The Goodheart-Willcox Co., South Holland, Illinois.

Walker, John R., EXPLORING METALWORKING, The Goodheart-Willcox Co., South Holland, Illinois.

Walker, John R., MACHINING FUNDAMENTALS, The Goodheart-Willcox Co., South Holland, Illinois.

Walker, John R., METAL PROJECTS BOOK 1, The Goodheart-Willcox Co., South Holland, Illinois.

Walker, John R., MODERN METALWORKING, The Goodheart-Willcox Co., South Holland, Illinois.

Acknowledgments

The author wishes to express his sincere appreciation to these associates in the Kansas City, Missouri, Public School system, for their assistance and contributions:

V. L. Pickens, Asst. Supt. in Charge of Practical Arts; Earl W. Boucher, Jr., drafting teacher, Central High School; Bernard E. Brightwell, metalwork teacher, Van Horn High School; Bernard G. Barisas, woodworking teacher, Southeast High School; Roy M. Carter, metalwork teacher, Southeast High School; Edwin W. Hamilton, metalwork teacher, Central High School; Marvin J. Nuernberger, Industrial Arts teacher, Bingham Junior High School.

Special credit is also due to the following companies for the generous supply of photographs, drawings, and information specifically provided for the preparation of this book.

Bridgeport Machines, Inc., Bridgeport, Conn.; Butler Mfg. Co., Kansas City, Mo.; The Cincinnati Milling Machine Co., Cincinnati, Ohio; The Cleveland Twist Drill Co., Cleveland, Ohio; Delta Power Tool Div., Rockwell Mfg. Co., Pittsburgh, Pa.; Ford Motor Co., Detroit, Mich.; Greenfield Tap & Die, Greenfield, Mass.; Johnson Gas Appliance Co., Cedar Rapids, Iowa; Nicholson File Co., Providence, R.I.; The Peck, Stow & Wilcox Co., Southington, Conn.; South Bend Lathe, Inc., South Bend, Ind.; Stanley Tools, New Britain, Conn.; The L. S. Starrett Co., Athol, Mass.; J. Wiss and Sons Co., Newark, N. J.

CONVERSION TABLE
METRIC TO ENGLISH

WHEN YOU KNOW: ⬇	MULTIPLY BY: * = Exact		TO FIND: ⬇
	VERY ACCURATE	APPROXIMATE	
LENGTH			
millimeters	0.0393701	0.04	inches
centimeters	0.3937008	0.4	inches
meters	3.280840	3.3	feet
meters	1.093613	1.1	yards
kilometers	0.621371	0.6	miles
WEIGHT			
grains	0.00228571	0.0023	ounces
grams	0.03527396	0.035	ounces
kilograms	2.204623	2.2	pounds
tonnes	1.1023113	1.1	short tons
VOLUME			
milliliters		0.2	teaspoons
milliliters	0.06667	0.067	tablespoon
milliliters	0.03381402	0.03	fluid ounces
liters	61.02374	61.024	cubic inches
liters	2.113376	2.1	pints
liters	1.056688	1.06	quarts
liters	0.26417205	0.26	gallons
liters	0.03531467	0.35	cubic feet
cubic meters	61023.74	61023.7	cubic inches
cubic meters	35.31467	35.0	cubic feet
cubic meters	1.3079506	1.3	cubic yards
cubic meters	264.17205	264.0	gallons
AREA			
square centimeters	0.1550003	0.16	square inches
square centimeters	0.00107639	0.001	square feet
square meters	10.76391	10.8	square feet
square meters	1.195990	1.2	square yards
square kilometers		0.4	square miles
hectares	2.471054	2.5	acres
TEMPERATURE			
Celsius	*9/5 (then add 32)		Fahrenheit

CONVERSION TABLE
ENGLISH TO METRIC

WHEN YOU KNOW: ⬇	MULTIPLY BY: * = Exact		TO FIND: ⬇
	VERY ACCURATE	APPROXIMATE	
LENGTH			
inches	* 25.4		millimeters
inches	* 2.54		centimeters
feet	* 0.3048		meters
feet	* 30.48		centimeters
yards	* 0.9144	0.9	meters
miles	* 1.609344	1.6	kilometers
WEIGHT			
grains	15.43236	15.4	grams
ounces	* 28.349523125	28.0	grams
ounces	* 0.028349523125	.028	kilograms
pounds	* 0.45359237	0.45	kilograms
short ton	* 0.90718474	0.9	tonnes
VOLUME			
teaspoon		5.0	milliliters
tablespoon		15.0	milliliters
fluid ounces	29.57353	30.0	milliliters
cups		0.24	liters
pints	* 0.473176473	0.47	liters
quarts	* 0.946352946	0.95	liters
gallons	* 3.785411784	3.8	liters
cubic inches	* 0.016387064	0.02	liters
cubic feet	* 0.028316846592	0.03	cubic meters
cubic yards	* 0.764554857984	0.76	cubic meters
AREA			
square inches	* 6.4516	6.5	square centimeter
square feet	* 0.09290304	0.09	square meters
square yards	* 0.83612736	0.8	square meters
square miles		2.6	square kilometer
acres	* 0.40468564224	0.4	hectares
TEMPERATURE			
Fahrenheit	* 5/9 (after subtracting 32)		Celsius

INDEX